Data Structures and Algorithms for Start-up People

Dr.M. Iyapparaja,

Associate Professor,

School of Information and Technology,

VIT University, Vellore.

Dr.A. Viswanathan,

Associate Professor,

Department of CSE,

K.S.R. College of Engineering, Tiruchengode

Published by

Data Structures and Algorithms for Start-up People

ISBN 978-93-86176-93-6

Authors

Dr.M. Iyapparaja

Dr.A. Viswanathan

Bonfring

309, 2nd Floor, 5th Street Extension, Gandhipuram,
Coimbatore-641 012.
Tamilnadu, India.
E-mail: info@bonfring.org
Website: www.bonfring.org
Phone: 0422 4213231

Dedicated to

My Parents, Wife & Children

Preface

This book offers the depth introduction to the different concepts of Data structures in C. This book means to oblige novices who hope to learning C and data structure under a similar umbrella. While showing C and data structure, we felt the requirement for an adjusted book regarding the matter. Truth be told, this is the principle driving force for composing such a book.

The mission for program proficiency requires not and ought not strife with sound outline and clears coding. Making effective projects has little to do with "programming traps" but instead depends on great association of data and great algorithms. A software engineer who has not aced the fundamental standards of clear plan is not liable to compose effective projects. On the other hand, "programming building" can't be utilized as a reason to legitimize wasteful execution. All inclusive statement in configuration can furthermore, ought to be accomplished without yielding execution, however this must be finished on the off chance that the creator sees how to gauge execution and does as such as an essential.

Our book trails five main nodes:

- Basics of Algorithms.
- Data Structures fundamentals.
- Sorting.
- Trees.
- Graphs and their applications.

The book is intended for a one-semester course or a one-year course. It is appropriate for courses in light of calculations and data structures. The essential for utilizing this content is rudimentary to centre level learning of C programming.

Dr.M. Iyapparaja

Author Profile

Dr.M. Iyapparaja, B.E., M.E., Ph.D., HDCA., MISTE.,

Associate Professor,

School of Information Technology & Engineering,

VIT University,

Vellore-632014.

Mobile: +91-9942532920

E-mail: iyapparaja.m@vit.ac.in,iyapparaja85@gmail.com

Dr.M. Iyapparaja received the Undergraduate Degree *B.E(Computer Science and Engineering) from the Anna University, Chennai.* He completed his master degree *M.E(Computer Science and Engineering) from the Anna University, Coimbatore. He received University Rank holder award for his PG Degree.* He completed his *Ph.D. Degree* in the area of "Risk Assessment in Software Engineering" from *Anna University, Chennai. He has 10 years of teaching experience.* He had completed *Honors Diploma in Computer Application course.* He is an *Associate Professor in School of Information Technology and Engineering, VIT University, Vellore.* He has *published 20 papers* in international, national journals and conference proceedings. He published two chapters in Scopus indexed publisher. His areas of research include Software Engineering, Agile Project Management, Big data and Data structures.

<table>
<tr><th>Unit</th><th>Contents</th><th>Page No</th></tr>
</table>

UNIT I

INTRODUCTION TO DATA STRUCTURES

Data structure is the most fundamental subject in engineering. It addresses the issue of organizing the data in most efficient manner. The study of data structure involves two things the specification of data structure and its implementation. Specification tells what kind of data structure is required and implementation tells us how the data structure can be used.

Problem Solving

In the computer science the big problem can be solved by building the algorithms. To solve any problem normally that problem is divided into sub problems and those sub problems are then solved. Then the solution of these sub problems is combined to obtain the solution of that main problem

There are two design approaches used in the problem-solving domain and those are

1) Top down design
2) Bottom up design

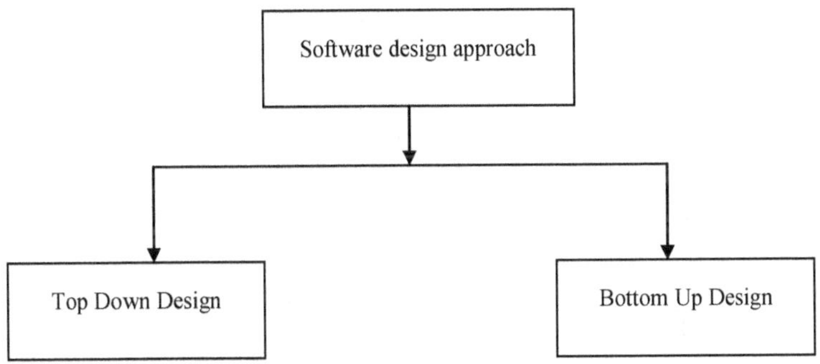

These software design strategies help a programmer to solve the complex problems efficiently.

Top Down Design

In top down design method a big global problem is divided into sub problems and these sub problems then can be solved to get the global solution. Usually in high-level languages the top down design approach is used to solve any problem. The figure below shows the top down design approach.

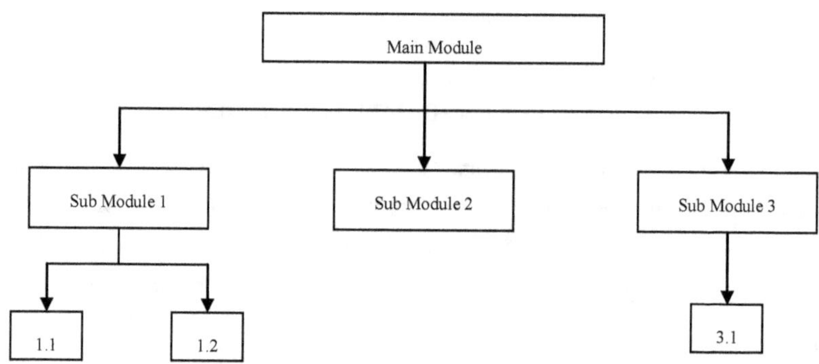

For example if we want to find the sum of two numbers then we can solve this problem by using top down design method as follows.

/*program for implementation of top down design method. This program is for addition of two numbers*/

```
#include<stdio.h>
#include<conio.h>
int a,b,c,sum;
void getthetwo_num();
int addoftwo_num();
void print_result(int);
void main()
{
clrscr();
printf("\n addition of two num");
getthetwo_num();
addoftwo_num();
print_result(c);
getch();
}
void getthetwo_num()
{
printf("\n enter the value for a:");
scanf("%d ",&a)
printf("\n enter the value for b:");
scanf("%d",&b);
```

```c
}
int addoftwo_num()
{
c=a+b;
return c;
}
void print_result(int c)
{
printf("the addition of two number is:%d",c);
}
```

Output

addition of two num

enter the value for a:3

enter the value for b:3

the addition of two number is:6

In the above program we are first writing the main function which act as a main function module, this main function is to solve the problem of addition of two numbers. And to accomplish this task the sub tasks are

1) Accepting of two numbers.
2) Performing two numbers.
3) Printing the addition of two numbers.
4) And for every sub task we have written functions. Thus the top down design approach is implemented.

Bottom Up Design

In the bottom up design method the modules are first created and these modules then are integrated to form a solution of big module or problem. The figure below represents the bottom up design approach.

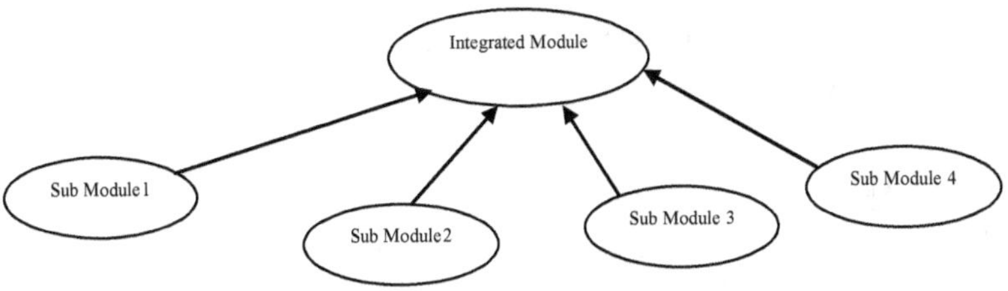

For example if we want to find the sum of two numbers then we can solve this problem by using bottom up design method as follows.

```c
/* this program is for implementing the bottom
up design for the program of addition of two numbers*/
#include<stdio.h>
#include<conio.h>
/*get_num function for accepting the two numbers*/
void get_num(int *x,int *y)
{
printf("\n enter the two numbers");
scanf("%d%d",x,y);
}
/* this sum function is for performing addition of two numbers*/
int sum(int a, int b)
{
int c;
c=a+b;
return c;
}
/* this print_ans function is for printing the addition as aresult*/
void print_ans(int z)
{
printf("the addition of two number=%d",z);
}
/*integrated module can be given by main function*/
void main()
{
int a,b,c;
clrscr();
printf("\n program for addition of two numbers:");
get_num(&a,&b);
c=sum(a,b);
print_ans(c);
getch(); }
```

Output

program for addition of two numbers:

enter the two numbers

6

6

The addition of two number=12

Algorithmic Analysis

An algorithm is a finite set of instructions for performing a particular task. The instructions are nothing but the statement in simple English language.

Example:

Let us take a very simple example of an algorithm which adds the two numbers and the result in a third variable.

Step 1: Start.
Step 2: read the first number in variable 'a'
Step 3: Read the second number in variable b
Step 4: perform the addition of both the numbers and store the result in variable 'c'
Step 5: print the value of 'c' as a result of addition.
Step 6: Stop.

Characteristics of Algorithm

1) Each algorithm is supplied with zero are external quantities. Here supplying external quantities means giving input to the algorithm.
2) Each algorithm must produce at least one quantity. Production of one quantity means there should be some output.
3) Each algorithm should have definiteness i.e. each instruction must be clear and unambiguous.
4) Each algorithm should have finiteness i.e. if we trace out the instructions of an algorithm, then for all cases the algorithm will terminate after finite number of steps.
5) Each algorithm should have effectiveness.

We need to distinguish between an algorithm and a program. The major difference is that algorithm always terminates while a program may not always terminate.

The efficiency of algorithm is directly related to the efficiency of program.

There are many criteria upon which we can judge program. For instance

1) Does my program work on what I want to do?
2) Does it work correctly according to original specifications?
3) Is the code readable?

The above criteria are important when one writes the software. Still there are other criteria for judging programs, which have a more direct relationship with performance. These are mainly concerned with computing time and storage requirements of the algorithms.

Suppose we want to find the time taken by following program statement.

$$X=x+1$$

If one ask the question that how much time it takes to execute this statement. It is impossible to determine exact time taken by the statement to execute unless we have the following information.

1) The machine that is used to execute this statement.
2) Machine language instruction set.
3) The time required by each machine instruction.
4) Compilation time (time taken by the compiler to make this statement to machine language).
5) And the kind of operating system (multi programming or time sharing).

Although, finding out the above-mentioned information is not difficult but this is not attractive option. The information may vary to machine to machine and perhaps we won't get the exact figures. So the better idea to determine the time taken by each instruction to execute is the frequency count.

Frequency Count

For example

1) x=x+1

    As this statement executes only once therefore the frequency count for this statement is 1.

2) for(I=0;I<n;I++)-this loop will be executed n times

    x=x+1;- this statement will be executed 1 time

    Above statement execute n times therefore the frequency count will be n. thus the performance of a program is measured in terms of "time complexity" i.e. total time taken by the algorithm to execute.

    Let us see more program fragments and have more discussion on frequency count.

Example 1

```
Main()
{
int j,n,a=10;
printf("\n Enter the value of n");
scanf("%d",&n);
for(j=0;j<n;j++)
a++;
}
```

Now let us analyse the above program fragment –

Concentrate on 'for' loop

1) j=0 will be executed one time

2) j<n will be executed n time i.e.

3) j++ will be executed n times

4) a++ will be executed n times.

Totally 1+(n+1)+n+n i.e. 3n+2

Generally when we sum the frequency count of all the statements in the given program we get a polynomial. However, for the sake of analysis we are interested in the order of magnitude of polynomial.

So we will drop the constant terms from the polynomial. Hence the order of magnitude is 'n' and it is denoted as O(n). "O" is called big-oh notation.

Example 2

```
Main()
{
                int j,k,n,a=10;
                printf("\n Enter the value of n");
                scanf("%d",&n);
                for(I=0;I<n;I++)
                {
                        for(k=0;k<n;k++)
                        {
                                a++;
                        }
                }
}
```

1. j=0 will be executed once.

2. the statement j<n will be executed n+1 times.

3. the frequency count for inner 'for' loop will be :

    k=0 once

    k<n n+1 times

    k++ n times

    a++ n times

    ____

    3n+2 i.e. n times

4. j will be incremented n times and the inner loop will be executed n times

    a. thus the total frequency count will be n*n i.e. n^2 times. There fore the frequency count for the above program will be n^2 and will be denoted as $O(n^2)$.

How to Choose Best Algorithm?

If we have two algorithms that perform same task, and the first one has a computing time of $O(n)$ and the second of $O(n^2)$, then we will usually prefer the first one.

The reason for this is that as n increases the time required for the execution of second algorithm will get far more than the time required for the execution of first. We will study various for computing function for the constant values. The graph given below will indicate the rate of growth of common computing time functions.

N	$Log_2 n$	$N \log_2 n$	N^2	N^3	2^n
1	0	0	1	1	2
2	1	2	4	8	4
4	2	8	16	64	16
8	3	24	64	512	256
16	4	64	256	4096	65536
32	5	160	1024	32768	4294967296

Notice how the times $O(n)$ and $O(nlogn)$ grow much more slowly than the others. For large data sets algorithms with a complexity greater than $O(nlogn)$ are often impractical. The very slow algorithm will be the one having the time complexity 2^n.

Asymptotic Notations

There are basically three types of mathematical notations for three different cases of time complexities.

1. Big oh or oh notation denoted as 'O'.

2. Omega notation denoted as Ω.

3. Theta notation denoted as θ.

Let us see one by one each notation.

1. Definition of big-oh notation

$$F(n) = O(g(n))$$

This means that always O(n) will give maximum amounts of time algorithm needs. I.e. O(n) gives "upper bound" on the time complexity value for the algorithm.

2. Definition of omega notation

$$f(n) = \Omega(g(n))$$

This means that always $\Omega(n)$ will give minimum amount of time the algorithm needs i.e. it gives "lower bound" on the time complexity value for the algorithm.

3. Definition of theta notation

$$f(n) = \theta(g(n))$$

This means that both upper bound and lower bound on f(n). I.e. worst and best cases require the same amount of time to within constant factor.

Examples of Asymptotic Notations

1) Big-oh and Omega Notation

Consider, an algorithm to search for a specific number from a set of n numbers we get two different time complexities.

One is for the best case and other is for the worst case. The best case for the algorithm is when the element to be searched is the one, which is stored at very first location. The worst case is when the number to be searched is placed at the end of the list. Thus in the best case only one comparison is needed while as in the worst-case n comparisons are needed. The best case as the time complexity as $\Omega(n)=1$ while the time complexity in the worst case will be O(n)=n.

2) Theta Notation

This indicates the lower and upper bound frequency. As an example consider an algorithm for finding out smallest number from a set of n numbers. Clearly this algorithm has identical for best and worst case time complexities. To find the smallest number from given list the maximum time required to scan the list and the minimum time required to scan the list will be the same. Clearly the time complexity of this algorithm is both O(n) and $\Omega(n)$ so we now represents the time complexity of this algorithm as $\theta(n)$.

Space Complexity

Another useful measure of an algorithm is the amount of storage space it needs. The space complexity of an algorithm can be computed by considering the data and their sizes. Again we are concerned with those data items, which demand for maximum storage space. A similar notation 'O' is used to denote the space complexity of an algorithm. When computing for storage requirement we assume each data element needs one unit of storage space. While as the aggregate data elements in an array this assumption again is independent of the machines on which the algorithms are to be executed.

UNIT II

LIST

Implementation of data structure can be done with help of programs. To write any program we need an algorithm. Algorithm is nothing but collection of instruction which ahs to be executed in step by step manner. And data structure tells us the way to organize data. To write any program we have to select proper algorithm and data structure. If we choose improper data structure, algorithm cannot work effectively. Thus there is a strong relationship between data structure and algorithm.

The following figure shows the classification of data structure.

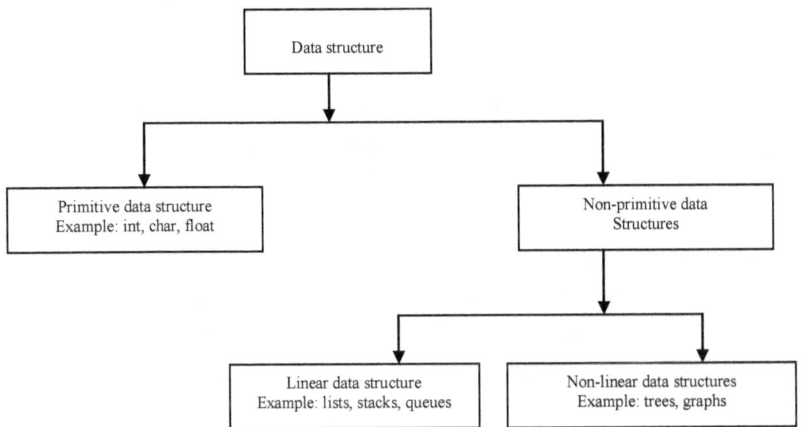

The list is the simplest data structure which represents the linear or sequential data structure. list, stacks and queues are also called as non primitive data structures. Data structures can also be categorized as primitive and non primitive data structures. Data structure which defines the non-primitive data structures are called primitive data structures. For example: integer, character, double, float. With the help of these data structures we can build list, stacks, queues.

Concept of Lists

List means collection of elements in sequential order. In memory we can store the list in two ways, one way is we can store the element in sequential memory locations. This is known as arrays. And the other way is we can use pointers or links to associate the elements in sequentially. This is known as linked lists.

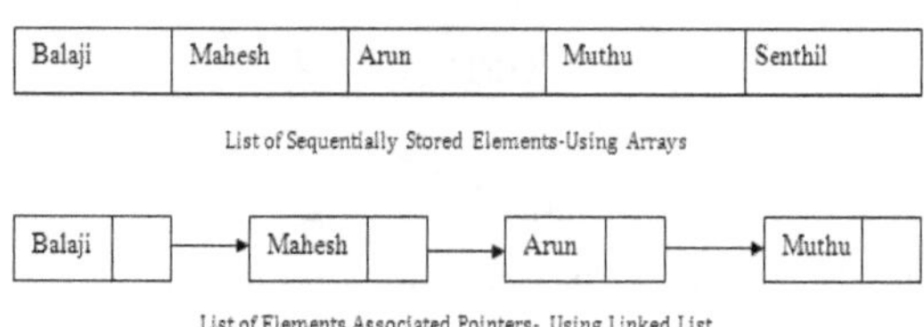

Arrays

An array is a collection of elements of similar data type. This collection is finite. And the elements are stored at adjacent memory locations. Thus array has to be finite in nature i.e. the size of the array should be specified.

For example: an array of 5 numbers-means the array size should not be less than 5 as well as the elements are numbers (either all are integer values are floating type values but not both).

Thus we can say array of n number of elements. Remember usually array elements are starting from 0th location; hence n number of elements can be counted from 0 to n-1. (No doubt, even we can store the elements from any location) the range of array is between a[0] to a[n-1]. (Here a is name of array). Range means total number of elements in the array. All these elements are always stored at contiguous memory locations. Any element of the array can be represented using index and name of the array. That means-a[0] represents the value stored at 0th location of the array, a[2] represents the value stored at 2nd location of the array and so on.

The syntax for array declaration is:

Data type array_name[size_of_array];

For example: int a[6]

The array a of size 6, has all the elements which are of integer type.

$$a[6]$$

Name	index
of the	of
Array	location

Let us understand such arrangement of array elements by following figure

a[0]	a[1]	a[2]	a[3]	a[4]	a[5]	a[6]
10	20	30	40	50	60	70

Types of Arrays

The arrays can be categorized as

1.   One dimensional arrays
2.   Multidimensional arrays.

One Dimensional Array

They are called one-dimensional because the data can be viewed entirely in one dimension. What that means is that you can think of the data in the array as being essentially one long chain. As we will see in the next topic, arrays can also extend to 2 dimensions, 3 dimensions, or any number of dimensions that you choose.

The effect that the dimensions have on accessing the data is that one index number is needed for each dimension.

In a one-dimensional array we can think of the single index as being an element's location in the list.

Example program for one dimensional array

```
/*searching a number*/
#include<stdio.h>
#include<conio.h>
void main()
{
int a[20],i,count,n,x,b;
clrscr();
printf("\n eneter the number of elements:");
scanf("%d",&n);
printf("\n enter the array elements:");
for(i=0;i<n;i++)/*accepting the values in the array using for loop*/
{
scanf("%d",&a[i]);
}
printf("\n enter the element u want to search:");
scanf("%d",&x);
for(i=0;i<n;i++)  /* searching the number using for loop*/
{
```

```c
if(x==a[i])
{
count=1;
b=i;
}
}
if(count==1)
printf("match found and the element is stored in %d position:",b);
else
printf("match not found:");
getch();
}
```

Output 1:

```
enter the number of elements:3
enter the array elements:10
20
30
enter the element u want to search:10
match found and the element is stored in 0 position:
```

Output 2:

```
enter the number of elements:3
enter the array elements:10
20
30
enter the element u want to search:40
match not found:
```

Two Dimensional Arrays

In two dimensional array the elements are stored in rows and columns. Thus to denote rows and columns we required two indices for the array. With the help of the indices we can decide at which position the element is stored in the array. The following figure shows how elements can be stored in two dimensional arrays.

	Col0	Col1	Col2
Row0	10 (0,0)	20 (0,1)	30 (0,2)
Row1	40 (1,0)	50 (1,1)	60 (1,2)
Row2	70 (2,0)	80 (2,1)	90 (2,2)

The above array is a[3][3] i.e. of total size of row is 3 and total size of columns is 3. if we want to access the element at position a[2][1] then that will be = 80

The two dimensional array is also called matrix because they represent the structure of matrix.

Example program for two dimensional array

```c
/* addition of two matrices*/
#include<stdio.h>
#include<conio.h>
#include<math.h>
void main()
{
int a[20][20],b[20][20],c[20][20],i,j,n;
clrscr();
printf("enter the order of the matrix:");
scanf("%d",&n);
for(i=0;i<n;i++) /*getting the values of a matrix*/
for(j=0;j<n;j++)
{
printf("enter the element for a position %d%d :",i,j);
scanf("%d",&a[i][j]);
}
for(i=0;i<n;i++) /*getting the values of b matric*/
for(j=0;j<n;j++)
{
printf("\n enter the element for position %d%d :",i,j);
scanf("%d",&b[i][j]);
}
```

```c
for(i=0;i<n;i++) /*adding a mtrix with b*/
for(j=0;j<n;j++)
{
c[i][j]=0;
c[i][j]=a[i][j]+b[i][j];
}
printf("\n the addition of two matrix a and b: is");
for(i=0;i<n;i++) /* printing the resultant matrix*/
{
printf("\n");
for(j=0;j<n;j++)
{
printf("\t%d",c[i][j]);
}
}
getch();
}
```

Output:

enter the order of the matrix:2

enter the element for a matrix position 00 :1

enter the element for a matrix position 01 :1

enter the element for a matrix position 10 :1

enter the element for a matrix position 11 :1

enter the element for b matrix position 00 :1

enter the element for b matrix position 01 :1

enter the element for b matrix position 10 :1

enter the element for b matrix position 11 :1

the addition of two matrix a and b is:

    2   2

    2   2

Linked List

Array is a static representation of list and linked list is a dynamic representation of list. Here static means that in arrays the number of elements is limited to the size of the array. If, total number of elements those are to be stored in the array are very few then the space in the array gets wasted. And dynamic means that as per memory requirement we can allocate the space or we can de-allocate the memory.

In the array the elements are stored in the adjacent memory locations but this is not the condition in the case of linked list. We can define linked list as a collection of similar data items, which are stored in the nodes. Here is a linked node.

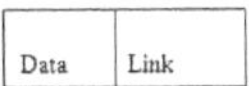

And these nodes form a linked list as follows.

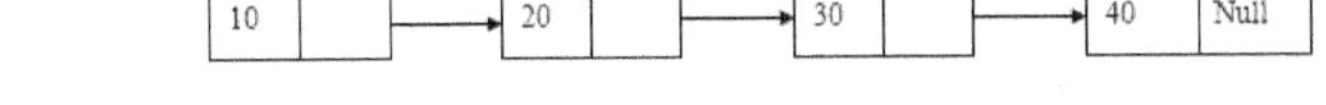


```c
/*implementation of linked list*/
#include<stdio.h>
#include<conio.h>
typedef struct NODE
{
int data;
struct NODE *next;
}node;
node n1,n2,n3,n4;
node *one,*temp;
void main()
{
clrscr();
n1.data=10;
n1.next=&n2;
n2.data=20;
n2.next=&n3;
n3.data=30;
n3.next=&n4;
n4.data=40;
```

```c
n4.next=NULL;
one=&n1;
temp=one;
while(temp!=NULL)
{
printf("\n%d",temp->data);
temp=temp->next;
}
getch();
}
```

Output:

10

20

30

40

Advantages of Linked List Over Arrays

As we know the basic draw back of static memory and array is management of memory. In both the cases either we create unnecessary extra memory or we get lack of memory. For example if array size we have declared is 50 and we have utilized only 10 locations then rest of the 40 locations get wasted or even reverse can be the situation that means there may be a case that we have to store 100 elements then we have to change the array size from 50 to at least 100. Of course this is to be poor space utilization. So there is a concept called dynamic memory management which came into picture for proper utilization of memory.

In computer world the two words 'static' and 'dynamic' have great importance. The static refers to an activity which is carried out at the time of compilation of a program and before execution of the program whereas dynamic means the activity carried out while the program is executed.

The static memory management means allocating/deallocating of memory at compilation time while the word refers to allocation/deallocation of memory while program is running. The advantage of dynamic memory management in handling the linked list is that we can create as many nodes as we desire and if some nodes are not required we can deallocate them. Such a dealliocated memory can be reallocated for some other nodes. Thus the scheme results in 100% memory utilization.

Dynamic Memory Management in C

In C language for allocating the memory dynamically 'malloc' function is used we should include alloc.h file in our program to support 'malloc'. Similarly for deallocating the memory 'free' function is used.

Types of Linked List

There are various types of linked list such as

1. Singly linear linked list.
2. Singly circular linked list.
3. Doubly linear linked list.
4. Doubly circular linked list.

Singly Linear Linked List

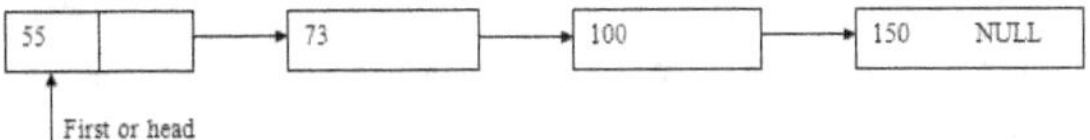

It is called singly because this list consists of only one link, to point to next node or element. This is also called linear list because the last element points to nothing it is linear in nature. The last field of last node is NULL which means that there is no further list. The very first node is called head or first.

Singly Circular Linked List

In this type of linked list only one link is used to point to next element and this list is circular means that the last node's link field points to be the first or head node. That means according to example after 100 the next number will be 25.So the list is circular in nature.

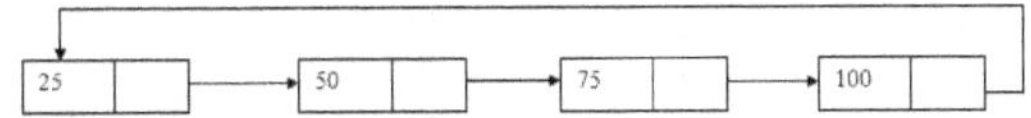

Doubly Linear Linked List

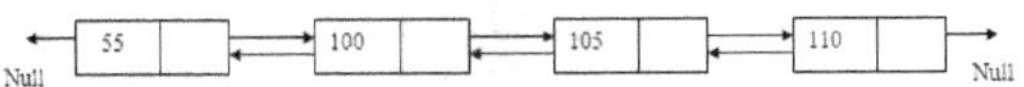

The list called doubly because each node has two pointers previous end and next pointers. The previous pointer points to previous node and next pointer points to next node. Only in the case of head node the previous pointer is obviously NULL and last node's next pointer points to NULL. This list is a linear one.

Doubly Circular Linked List

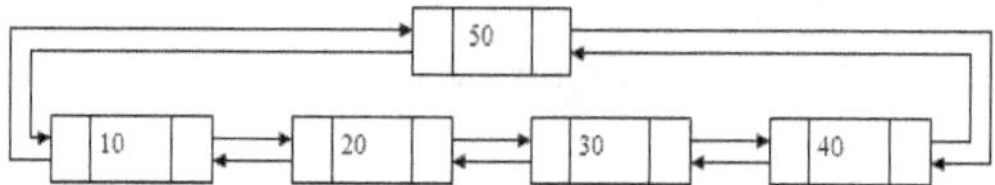

In circular doubly linked list the previous pointer of first node and the next pointer of last node is pointed to head node. Head node is a special node which may have any dummy data or it may have some useful information such as total number of nodes in the list which may be used to simplify the algorithms carrying various operations on the list.

Stack

The stack is an ordered list but the insertions and deletions are restricted by certain rules. For example, in a stack the operations are carried out in a way such that the last element which is inserted will be the first one to come out. Such a order is called last in first out or LIFO. The ordered list does not have such specific ordering and the elements can be inserted and deleted in any random order. Thus the stack may be treated as special case of ordered list.

Now the most important question which arises is that, what is the notation of such specific ordering such as LIFO? Consider a book shelf which is closed form all the sides except the top. How do we keep books onto such a shelf? The only way to arrange one book over other. Now how can we remove a book from it? The only way is to remove all the books, one at a time from the top till the book which we want is removed. So if we want to remove the most recently stacked book, it will be at the top most position and can be removed immediately. On the other hand, if we want to remove the book which we have stacked at the very first time, then we will have to remove all the books which are stacked on top of it, one book at a time. clearly this is an example of last in first out LIFO structure. In computer science, many of the problems can be solved by using a LIFO ordering, i.e. by using stacks. Stacks are used for expression conversion during compilation.

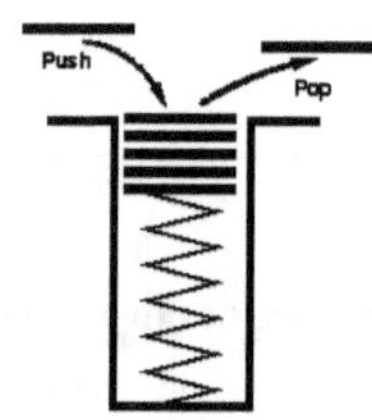

The above figure shows the block diagram of stack

Representation of Stack

A stack is a special case of an ordered list, i.e. it is a ordered list with some restrictions on the way in which we perform various operations on a list. It is therefore quite natural to use sequential representation for implementing a stack.. to do this, we need to define an array of some maximum size. Moreover, we need an integer variable top which will keep track of the top of the stack as more and more elements are inserted into and deleted from the stack. The declarations in C are as follows

Declaration 1

```
#define size 100
int stack[size],top=-1;
```

In the above declaration we assume that the elements in the stack are integers and so we will refer to such a stack as integer stack. This stack is capable of storing size number of elements. As we have given # define size 100. the very first element will be at position stack[0], the next at stack[1] and so on. The last element is at position stack[size-1].

Declaration 2

```
#define size 10
struct stack {
int s[size];
int top;
}st;
```

Now compare declaration 1 and 2. both are for stack declaration only. But the second declaration will be always preferred on why? Because in the second declaration we have used a structure for stack elements and top. By this we are binding or co-relating top variable with stack elements. Thus top and stack are associated with each other by putting them together in a structure. The stack can be passed to the function by simply passing the structure variable. we will make use of the second method of representing the stack in our program.

Stack Empty Operation

Initially stack is empty. And that time the top should be initialized to -1 or 0. if we set top to -1 initially then the stack will contain the elements from 0th position and if we set top to 0 initially, the elements will be stored from 1st position, in the stack.. elements may be pushed onto the stack and there may be a case that all the elements are removed from the stack. Then the stack becomes empty. Thus whenever top reaches to -1 we can say the stack is empty.

Int stempty()

{

if(st.top==-1)

return 1;

else

return 0;

}

Stack Full Operation

When we create a stack using sequential representation, we need to fix the maximum size of it. We then can go on inserting elements into stack up to this maximum limit. So every time, to insert an element into the stack, we must check whether the stack is full or not. if it is full then we cannot insert an element. So we need a mechanism to decide whether the stack is full or not and it is as shown below.

Int stfull()

{

if(st.top>=size-1)

return 1;

else

return 0;

}

The 'stfull' is a boolean function, which returns 1 if there is no more room to accommodate a new element and returns 0 otherwise. Note that the original value of top is not modified. The top of the stack will be compared with the maximum size –1, since the array starts placing the elements from 0th position.

The 'Push' and 'Pop' Function

We will now discuss the two important functions which are carried out on a stack.. push is a function which inserts new element at the top of the stack. The function is as follows.

Void push(int item)

{

st.top++;

st.s[st.tp]=item;

}

note that the push function takes the parameter item which is actually the element which we want to insert into the stack means we are pushing the element onto the stack. In the function we have checked wheather the stack is full or not, if the stack is not full then the insertion of the elements can be achieved by means of push operation

Now let us discuss the operation pop, which deletes the element at the top of the stack. The function pop is given as follows.

```
Int pop()
{
int item;
item = st.s[st.top];
st.top--;
return(item);
}
```

in the choice of pop it invokes the function 'stempty' to determine whether the stack is empty or not. If it is empty, then the function generates an error as stack underflow ! If not, then pop function returns the element which is at the top of the stack. The vale at the top is stored in some variable as item and it then decrements the value of the top, which now points to the element which is just under the element being retrieved from the stack..

Finally it returns the value of the element stored in the variable item. Note that this is called as logical deletion and not a physical deletion, i.e. even when we decrement the top, the element is just retrieved from the stack remains there Itself, but it no longer belongs to the stack. Any subsequent push will overwrite this element.

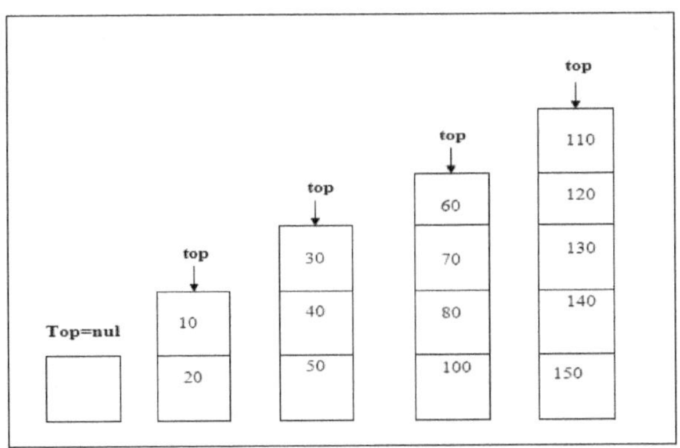

Pictorial Representation of Stack After Inserting Elements

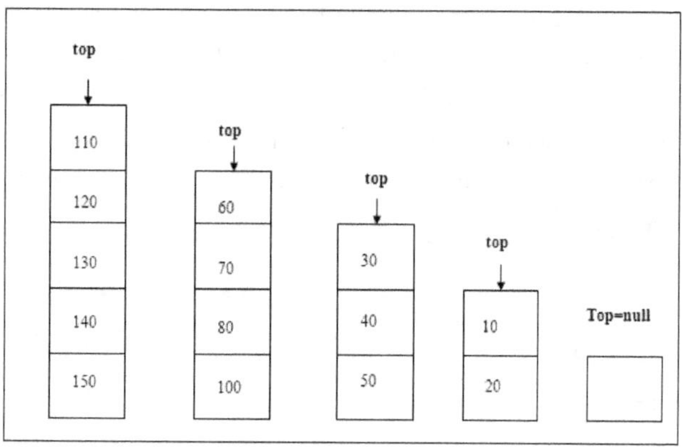

Pictorial Representation of Stack After Deletion of Stacks

Stack Implementation

```c
/*stack implementation*/
#include<stdio.h>
#include<conio.h>
#define size 10
struct stack
{
int s[size];
int top;
}st;
int stfull(void)
{
if(st.top==size-1)
return(1);
else
return(0);
}
void push(int item)
{
st.top++;
st.s[st.top]=item;
}
```

```c
int stempty(void)
{
if(st.top==-1)
return(1);
else
return(0);
}
int pop()
{
int item;
item=st.s[st.top];
st.top--;
return(item);
}
void display()
{
int i;
if(stempty())
printf("stack is empty:");
else
for(i=st.top;i>=0;i--)
{
printf("%d",st.s[i]);
}
}
void main(void)
{
int choice,item;
char ans;
st.top=-1;
clrscr();
do
{
printf("\n 1.push \n 2.pop\n 3.display\n 4.exit");
```

```c
printf("\n enter your choice:");
scanf("%d",&choice);
switch(choice)
{
case 1:
printf("enter the item u want to push:");
scanf("%d",&item);
if(stfull())
printf("stack is full:");
else
push(item);
break;
case 2:
if(stempty())
printf("stack is empty:");
else
{
item=pop();
printf("the poped element is%d",item);
}
break;
case 3:
display();
break;
case 4:
exit(0);
}
printf("\n do u want to continue?");
ans=getche();
}
while(ans=='y');
getch();
}
```

Output:

1.push

2.pop

3.display

4.exit

enter your choice:1

enter the item u want to push:10

do u want to continue? y

1.push

2.pop

3.display

4.exit

enter your choice:1

enter the item u want to push:20

do u want to continue? y

1.push

2.pop

3.display

4.exit

enter your choice:1

enter the item u want to push:30

do u want to continue? y

1.push

2.pop

3.display

4.exit

enter your choice:3

30

20

10

do u want to continue? y

1.push

2.pop

3.display

4.exit

enter your choice:2

the poped element is30

do u want to continue?y

1.push

2.pop

3.display

4.exit

enter your choice:2

the poped element is20

do u want to continue? y

1.push

2.pop

3.display

4.exit

enter your choice:2

the poped element is10

 do u want to continue?y

1.push

2.pop

3.display

4.exit

enter your choice:2

stack is empty:

do u want to continue? N

Applications of Stack

The place where stacks are frequently used is in expression conversion. An arithmetic expression consist of operands and operators. The operands can be numeric values or numeric variables. The operators used in an arithmetic expression represent the operations like addition, subtraction, multiplication, division and exponentiation.

Various applications of stack are

1. Expression conversion.
2. Expression evaluation.
3. Parsing well formed parenthesis.
4. Decimal to binary conversion.
5. Reversing a string.

One of the application of stack is conversion of expression. First of all let us see various types of expressions. There are three types of expressions

1) Infix Expression

In this type of expression the operator is in between the operands. which means that if we take + operator which is a binary operator then in infix type it will be operand operator operand i.e. infix expression: a + b where a and b are the operands and + is an operator.

2) Prefix Expression

In this type of expression the operator come first and then two operands can be placed. The way to write the prefix expression can be

Prefix expression=operator operand operand

For example the infix expression a + b can be written as +ab

3) Postfix Expression

In the postfix expression the operator should be written as last i.e. postfix expression = operand operand operator

For example the infix expression a+b can be written as ab+

Let us see few more examples

Infix	Postfix	Prefix
A + B * C	A B C * +	+ A * B C
(A + B) * C	A B + C *	* + A B C
A - B - C	A B - C -	- - A B C
A ^ B ^ C	A B C ^ ^	^ A B ^ C

Note that the prefix and postfix forms do not make use of parenthesis as these forms are unambiguous. The order of applying operators is unique. In the first example of postfix expression, the operators '*' and '+' appear after the operands. The expression will be evaluated by first applying the operator '*' on B and C and then apply '+' with a and the result. In case of prefix form, similar order can be extracted.

Converting an Expression from Infix into Postfix

Algorithm for Converting Infix into Postfix Expression

1. Scan the expression from left to right.
2. If any operands comes print it simply
3. If any operator comes compare the incoming operator with stack operator. If the incoming operator priority is higher than stack operator priority push the incoming operator.
4. If the incoming operator has less priority than the operator inside the stack then go on popping the operator from top of the stack and print them till this condition is true and then push the incoming operator on top of the stack.
5. If both incoming and stack operator priority are equal then pop the stack operator till this condition is true.
6. If the operator is ')' then go on popping the operators from top of the stack and print them till a matching '('operator is found. Delete '(' from top of the stack.

Let us take the example

Example 1: A * B + C $

Input	stack	Output
none	empty	none
A	empty	A
*	*	A
B	*	AB
+	Pop * and Push +	AB*
C	+	AB*C
$	empty	AB*C+

Example 2: A * (B + D) / E – F * (G + H / K)

Input	Stack	Output
A	none	A
*	*	A
(	(*	A
B	(*	AB
+	+(*	AB
D	+(*	ABD
)	* Pop + and delete (	ABD+
/	Pop * and push /	ABD+*
E	/	ABD+*E
-	Pop / and push -	ABD+E/
F	-	ABD+E/F
*	* -	ABD+E/F
(	(*-	ABD+E/F
G	(*-	ABD+E/FG
+	+(*-	ABD+E/FG
H	+(*-	ABD+E/FGH
/	/+(*-	ABD+E/FGH
K	/+(*-	ABD+E/FGHK
)	*- Pop /+ delete (	ABD+E/FGHK/+
None	Pop *-	ABD+E/FGHK/+*-

Converting an Expression from Infix into Prefix

Algorithm for Converting Infix into Prefix Expression

1. Reverse the given expression
2. Scan the expression from left to right.
3. If any operands comes print it simply
4. If any operator comes compare the incoming operator with stack operator. If the incoming operator priority is higher than stack operator priority push the incoming operator.
5. If the incoming operator has less priority than the operator inside the stack then go on popping the operator from top of the stack and print them till this condition is true and then push the incoming operator on top of the stack.
6. If both incoming and stack operator priority are equal then push the incoming operator.
7. If the operator is ')' then push the operator. Repeat the steps 3,4,5,6 for upcoming operators till a matching '('operator is found. then go on pop the operators from top of the stack and delete the ')' operator.

Let us take the example

Example 1: A * B + C $

Input	Stack	Output
A	None	A
*	*	A
B	*	AB
+	Pop * and push +	AB*
C	+	AB*C
$	$ +	AB*C
None	Pop $ +	AB*C$+

Queue

What is Queue?

The queue can be formally defined as ordered collection of elements that has two ends named as front and rear. From the front one can delete the elements and from the rear end one can insert the elements.

For Example

The typical example can be a queue of people who are waiting for a city bus at the bus stop. Any new person is joining at one end of the queue, you can call it as the rear end. When the bus arrives the person at the other end first enters in the bus. You can call it as the front end of the queue.

Following figure-represents the queue of few elements.

94	98	34	58	77	12	32	44

Front   Rear

Sequential Representation of Queue

Queue is nothing but the collection of items. Both the ends of the queue are having their own functionality. The queue is also called as FIFO i.e. First In First Out data structure. All the elements in the queue are stored sequentially. The various operations on the queue are

1. Queue Overflow.
2. Insertion of the element into the queue.
3. Queue Underflow.
4. Deletion of the element from the queue.
5. Display of the Queue.

Let us see each operation one by one.

1) Insertion of Element Into the Queue

The insertion of any element in the queue will always take place from the rear end. Before performing insert operation you must check whether the queue is full or not. If the rear pointer is going beyond the maximum size of the queue then the queue is overflow occurs

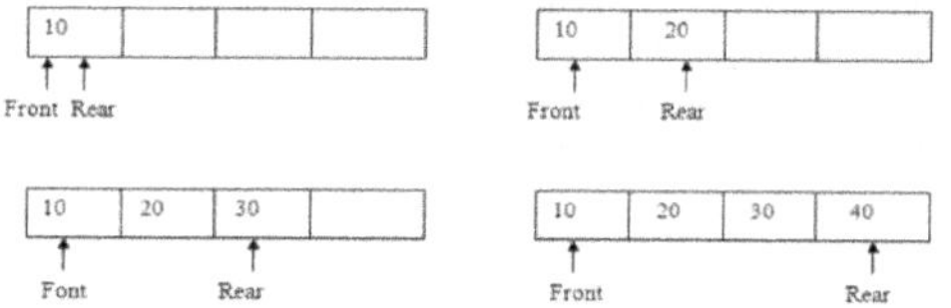

2) Deletion of Element from the Queue

The deletion of any element in the queue takes place by the front end always. Before performing any delete operation one must check whether the queue is empty or not. If the queue is empty, you cannot perform the deletion. The result of illegal attempt to delete an element from the empty queue is called the queue underflow condition.

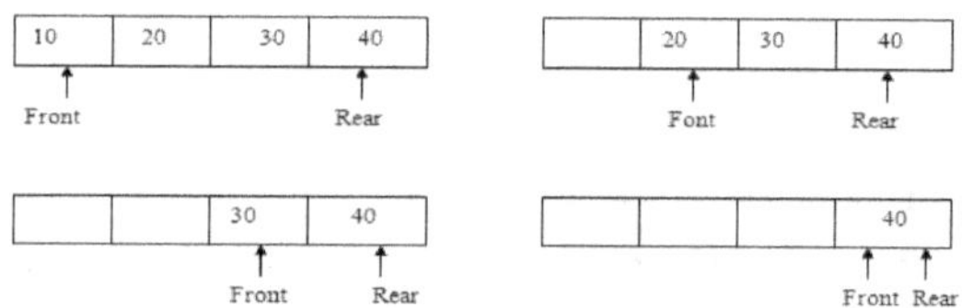

Queue Implementation

```c
/*Queue Implementation*/
#include<stdio.h>
#include<conio.h>
#define size 10
struct queue
{
int que[size];
int front,rear;
}q;
int full()
{
if(q.rear>=size-1)
return(1);
else
return(0);
}
int insert(int item)
{
if(q.front==-1)
q.front++;
q.que[++q.rear]=item;
return q.rear;
}
int empty()
{
if((q.front==-1)||(q.front>q.rear))
return(1);
else
return(0);
}
int delete()
{
int item;
```

```c
item=q.que[q.front];
q.front++;
printf("\n the deleted itemis%d",item);
return q.front;
}
void display()
{
int i;
for(i=q.front;i<=q.rear;i++)
printf("%d\n",q.que[i]);
}
void main(void)
{
int choice,item;
char ans;
clrscr();
q.front=-1;
q.rear=-1;
do
{
printf("\nmenu");
printf("\n 1.insert \n 2.delete \n 3.display");
printf("\n enter ur choice");
scanf("%d",&choice);
switch(choice)
{
case 1:
if(full())
printf("\n cannot insert element:");
else
{
printf("enter the item u wnat to insert:");
scanf("%d",&item);
insert(item);
```

```c
}
break;
case 2:
if(empty())
printf("\n queue is under flow:");
else
delete();
break;
case 3:
if(empty())
printf("queue is empty");
else;
display();
break;
}
printf("\n do u want to continue?");
ans=getche();
}
while(ans=='y');
}
```

Output:

```
menu
1.insert
2.delete
3.display
enter ur choice1
enter the item u wnat to insert:10
do u want to continue?y
menu
1.insert
2.delete
3.display
enter ur choice1
enter the item u wnat to insert:20
```

do u want to continue?y

menu

1.insert

2.delete

3.display

enter ur choice

enter the item u wnat to insert:30

do u want to continue?y

menu

1.insert

2.delete

3.display

enter ur choice3

10

20

30

do u want to continue?y

menu

1.insert

2.delete

3.display

enter ur choice2

the deleted itemis10

do u want to continue?y

menu

1.insert

2.delete

3.display

enter ur choice2

the deleted itemis20

do u want to continue?y

menu

1.insert

2.delete

3.display

enter ur choice2

the deleted itemis30

do u want to continue?y

menu

1.insert

2.delete

3.display

enter ur choice2

queue is under flow:

do u want to continue?n

Types of Queue

Circular Queue

In case of linear queue the elements get deleted logically. Following fig can show this

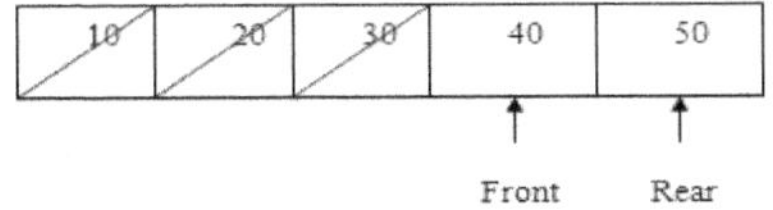

We have deleted the elements 10,20 and 30 means simply the rear pointer is shifted ahead. We will consider a queue from front to rear always. And now if we try to insert any more elements then it won't be possible as it is going to give "queue full" message. Although there is a space of elements 10,20 and 30 we cannot utilize them because queue is nothing but a linear array. Hence there is a concept called circular queue. The main advantage of circular queue is we can utilize the space of the queue fully. The circular queue is shown below.

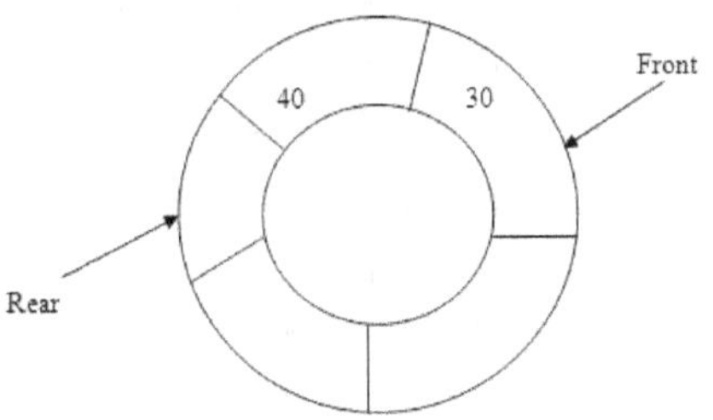

There is a formula which has to be applied for setting the front and rear pointers for a circular queue.

Rear = (rear+1) % size

Front = (front+1) % size

For example

Rear= (rear+1) %size

$\quad$ = (4+1) % 5

Rear=0

So we can store the element 60 at 0th location similarly while deleting the element

Front = (front+1) size

$\quad$ = (3+1) % 5 = 4

So delete the element at 4th location i.e. element 50.

Deque

The word Deque is a short form of double-ended queue and defines a data structure in which items can be added or deleted at either the front end or rear and, but no changes can be made elsewhere in the list. Thus a deque is a generalization of both a stack and a queue. Below figure show the representation of a deque.

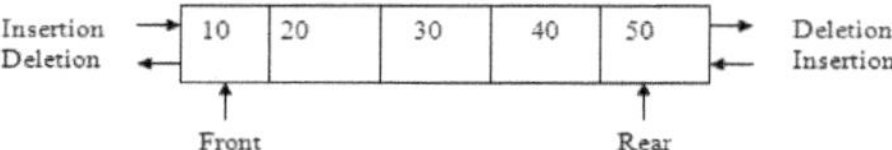

As we know, normally we insert the elements by rear and delete the elements from front end. Now if we wish to insert the element from front end then first we have to shift all the elements to the right. If one wishes to perform the deletion operation in the rear end simply decrement the rear pointer by one.

Priority Queue

A priority queue is a collection of elements where the elements are stored according to their priority levels. The order in which the elements should get added or removed is decided by the priority of the element. Following rules are applied to maintain a priority queue.

(a) The element with a higher priority is processed before any element of lower priority.

(b) If there are elements with the same priority, then the element added first in the queue would get processed first.

There are two types of priority queues

1. Ascending priority queue: it is a collection of item in which the items can be inserted arbitrarily but only the smallest element can be removed first.

2. Descending priority queue: it is a collection of item in which insertion of elements is an order but only the largest element can be removed first.

Applications of Priority Queue

Priority queues are used for implementing job scheduling by the operating system where jobs with higher priorities are to be processed first. Another application of priority queues is simulation systems where priority corresponds to event times.

Applications of Queue

There are various applications of queue such as

Josephus Problem

This is the application of the queue in which the circular queue is being used.

Job Scheduling

In the operating system various programs are getting executed.

We cal these programs as jobs. In this process, some programs are in executing state. The state of these programs is called as 'running' state. Some programs are not executing but they are in a position to get executed at any time such programs are in the 'ready' state. And there are certain programs which are neither in running state nor in ready state. Such programs are in a state called as blocked state.

The operating system maintains a queue of all such running state, ready state, blocked state programs. Thus use of queues help the operating system to schedule the jobs. The jobs which are in running state are removed after complex execution of each job, then the jobs which are in ready state change their state from ready to running and get entered in the queue for running state. Similarly the jobs which are in blocked state can change their state from blocked to ready state.

These jobs then can be entered in the queue for ready state jobs. Thus every job changes its states and finally get executed.

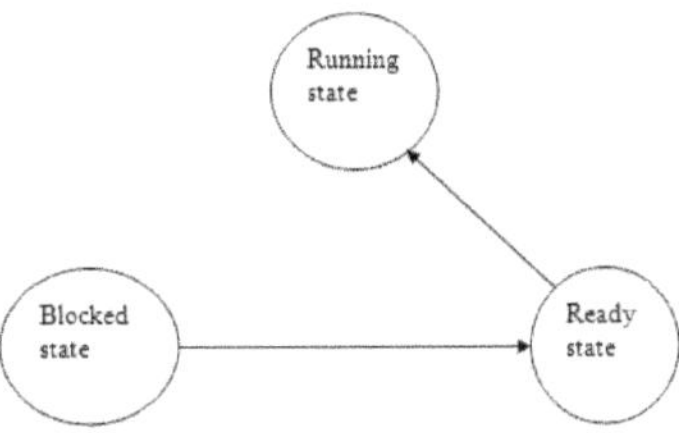

Abstract Data Type

In programming, a data type that is defined in terms of the information it can contain and the operations that can be performed with it. An abstract data type is more generalized than one constrained by the properties of the objects it contains – for example, the data type "pet" is more generalized than the data types "pet dog," "pet bird," and "pet fish." The standard example used in illustrating an abstract data type is the stack, a small portion of memory used to store information, generally on a temporary basis.

UNIT III

TREE

Nature is man's best teacher. In every walk of life man has looked and explored the nature, learnt his lessons and then applied the knowledge that nature offered him to solve every-day problems that he faced at work place. It isn't without reason that there are data structures like trees, binary trees, search trees, AVL trees, forests, etc.

The data structures that we have seen so for (such as linked lists, stack and queues) were linear data structures. As against this, trees are non-linear data structures.

In a linked list each node has a link which points to another node. In a tree structure, however, each node may points to several other nodes (which may then point to several other nodes). Thus tree is a very flexible and powerful data structure that can used for a wide variety of applications.

For example, an engineering college. Such a system has information which can be represented in hierarchical form in the most natural way. A college has n number of departments each for particular branch of engineering. In each department there are students studying in respective semester and there are teachers of various designations such as professor, assistant professors, lecturer. This information system is shown in tree form as below.

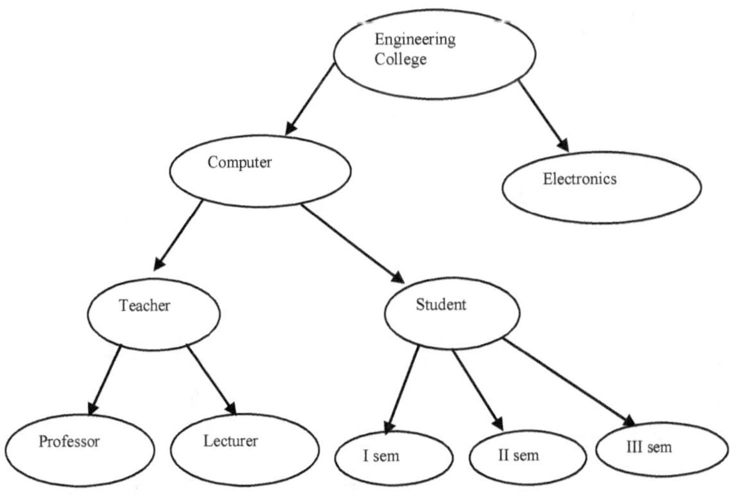

A Tree Structure

Definition of Tree

A tree is a finite set of one or more nodes such that

1) There is a specially designated node called root.

2) The remaining nodes are partitioned into n>=0 disjoint sets T1, T2, T3,...... Tn

Where T1, T2, T3,....Tn are called the sub trees of the root.

Representation of Tree

Basically tree is a set of nodes and every node consists of data. The data of the tree is some information which may be numeric or alphabetic. Each node may or may not have further sub-trees. One can visualize the tree like this

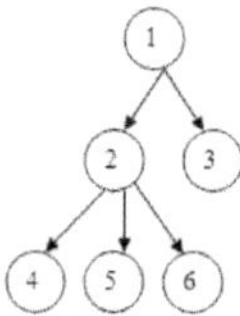

For each node in the tree structure there could be n+ fields

The calculation for n+1 nodes is as below

n – maximum number of branches attached to that node.

1 – data field indicating the information of that node.

Tree Terminology

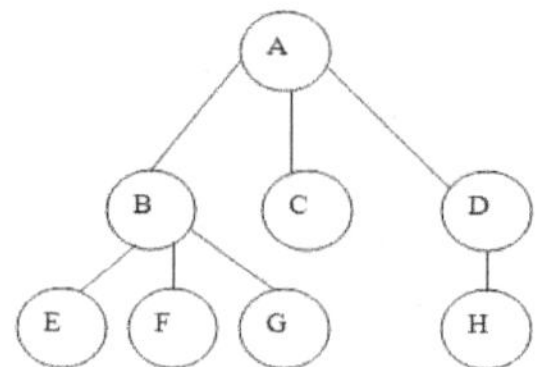

1) *Root*

This is the unique node in the tree to which further sub-trees are attached. In the figure A is a root node.

2) *Degree of the Node*

The total number of sub-trees attached to that node is called the degree of the node. For node A the degree is 3, for node E the degree is 0.

3) Leaves

These are the terminal nodes of the tree. The nodes with degree 0 always the leaves. Here in our example E,F,C,G,H are the leaf nodes.

4) Internal Nodes

The nodes other than the root node and the leaves are called the internal nodes. Here B and D are the internal nodes.

5) Parent Node

The node which is having further sub-branches is called the parent node of those sub-branches.

In the above figure the node B is parent node of E,F,G nodes. And E,F,G are called the children of the parent B.

6) Predecessor

While displaying the tree, if some particular node occurs previous to some other node then that node is called the predecessor of the other node. In our example the node E is predecessor of the node B.

7) Successor

The node, which occurs next to some other node. In our example B is a successor of F and G.

8) Level of the Tree

The root node is always considered at level zero, then its adjacent children are suppose to be at level 1 and so on.

In the above figure A is at level 0, the nodes B,C,D are at level 1, the nodes E,F,G,H, are at level 2.

9) Height of the Tree

The maximum level is the height of the tree. Here the height of the tree is 3. The other terminology used for height of the tree is depth of the tree.

10) Forest

A tree may be defined as a forest in which only a single node (root) has no predecessors. Any forest consists of collection of tree.

11) Degree of Node

The degree of each node is defined as the total number of sub-branches each node may have. The node A will have the degree 3.

12) Degree of Tree

The maximum degree of the node in the tree is called the degree of the tree.

Binary Trees

A binary tree consist of a finite set of elements that can be portioned into three distinct sub-sets called the root, the left and the right sub-tree. If there are no elements in the binary tree it is called an empty binary tree.

Types of Binary Trees

There are three types of binary trees

1) Left Skewed Binary Tree

If the right sub tree is missing in every node of a tree we call it as left skewed binary tree.

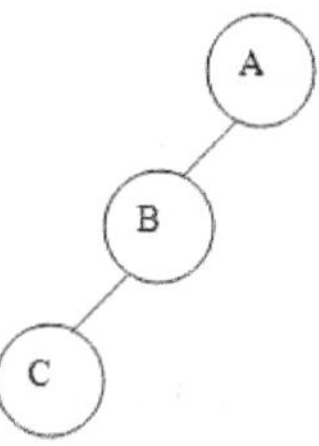

2) Right Skewed Binary Tree

If the left sub-tree is missing in every node of a tree we call it as right skewed binary tree.

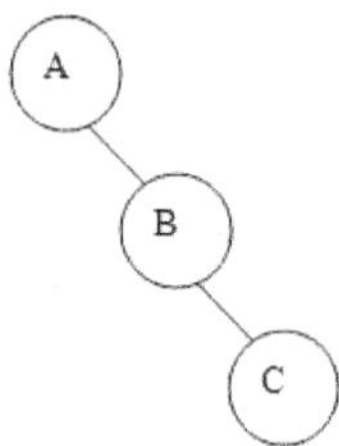

3) Complete Binary Tree

The tree in which degree of each node is at the most two is called a complete binary tree. In a complete binary tree there is exactly one node at level 0, two nodes at level 1 and four nodes at level 2 and so on. So we can say that a complete binary tree of depth d will contain exactly 2^l nodes at each level l, where L is from 0 to d.

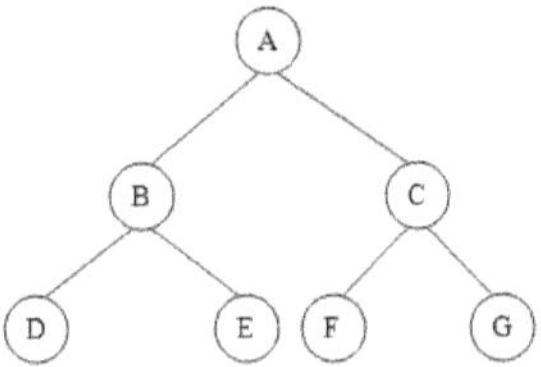

Binary Tree Representation

There are two ways of representing the binary tree.

1) Sequential Representation
2) Linked Representation

1) Sequential Representation

Each node is sequentially arranged from top to bottom and from left to right. Let us understand this matter by numbering each node. The numbering will start from root node and then remaining nodes will give ever increasing numbers in level wise direction. The node on the same level will be numbered from left to right. The numbering will be shown in figure.

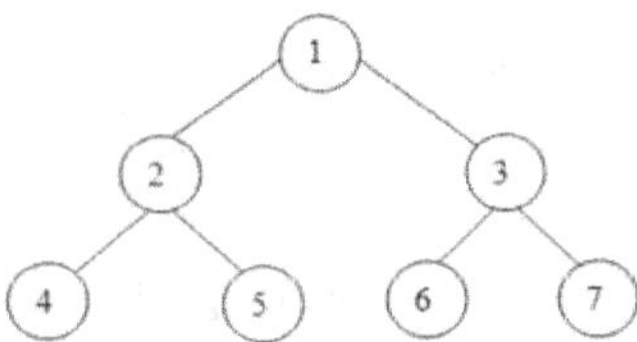

Now observe this figure carefully. You will get a point that a binary tree of depth n having 2^n-1 number of nodes. In this figure the tree is having the depth 3 and the total number of nodes are 7. thus remember that in a binary tree of depth n there will be maximum 2^n-1 nodes. And so if we know the maximum depth of the tree then we can represent binary tree using arrays data structure.

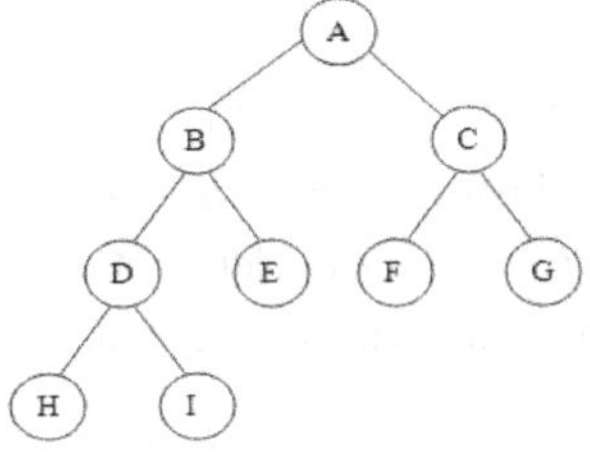

Root=A=index0

Left child of A i.e.. n=0

B will be at 2*0+1=1st location

Similarly right child of A which will be C

Therefore C will be at 2*0+2=2nd location

I is at 8th location

2n+2=8,2n=6,n=3

that means parent of I is at 3rd location and i.e. D.

Advantages of Sequential Representation

The only advantage with this type of representation is that the direct access to any node can be possible and finding the parent or left right children of any particular node is fast because of the random access.

Disadvantage of Sequential Representation

1) The major disadvantage with this type of representation is wastage of memory.

2) In this type of representation the maximum depth of the tree has to be fixed. Because we have to decide the array size. If we choose the array size quite larger than the depth of the tree, then it will be wastage of the memory. And if we choose array size lesser than the depth of the tree then we will be unable to represent some part of the tree.

3) The insertion and deletion of any node in the tree will be costlier as other nodes has to be adjusted at appropriate so that the meaning of binary tree can be preserved.

As these drawbacks are there with this sequential type of representation, we will search for more flexible representation. So instead of array we will make use of linked list to represent the tree.

2) Linked Representation

In linked list each node will look like this

Left Child	Data	Right Child

In binary tree each node will have left child, right child and data filed. The left child is nothing but the left link which points to some address of left sub-tree where as right child is also a right link which points to some address of right sub-tree. And the data filed gives the information about the node.

Advantages of Linked Representation

1) This representation is superior to our array representation as there is no wastage of memory. And so there is no need to have prior knowledge of depth of the tree using dynamic memory concept one can create as much memory as required. By chance if some nodes are unutilized one can delete the nodes by making the address free.

2) Insertions and deletions which are the most common operations can be done with out moving the other nodes.

Disadvantages of Linked Representation

1) This representation does not provide direct access to a node and special algorithms are required.

2) This representation needs additional space in each node for storing the left and right sub-trees.

Binary Tree Traversals

The traversal of binary tree involves visiting each node in the tree exactly once. In several applications involving binary tree we need to go to each node in the tree systematically. In a linear list, nodes can be visited in a systematic manner from beginning to end. However, such an order is not possible while traversing a tree. Basically there are six ways to traverse a tree. For these traversals we will use some notations as follows :

L means move to left child

R means move to right child

D means the root/parent node.

Now, with this L,R,D one can have six different combinations of L,R,D nodes.

Such as LDR, LRD, DLR, DRL, RLD, RDL. But form computing point of view we will have three different ways of traversing a tree. Those three combinations will be LDR, DLR, LRD. Those are called **in order, preorder, post order**. The methods differs primarily in the order in which they visit the root node the nodes in the left sub-tree and the nodes in the right sub-tree.

In Order Traversal

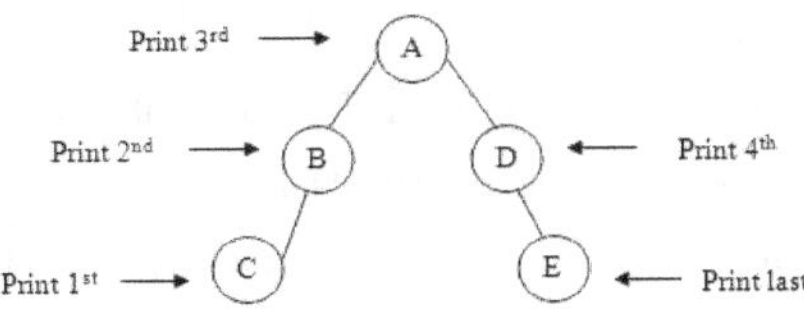

C-B-A-D-E is the in order traversal i.e. first we go towards the leftmost node i.e. C so print the node. Then back to the node B and print B. then root node A then move towards the right sub-tree print D and finally E. thus we are following the tracing sequence of LDR. This type of traversal is called in- order traversal. The basic principle is to traverse left sub-tree then root and then the right sub-tree.

Pre Order Traversal

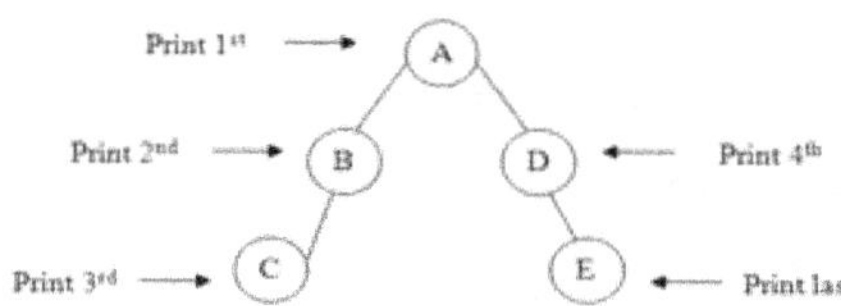

A-B-C-D-E is the pre order traversal of the above figure. We are following DLR path i.e. data at the root node will be printed first then we move on the left sub-tree and go on printing the data till we reach to the leftmost node. Print the data at that node and then move to the right sub-tree. Follow the same DLR principle at each sub-tree and go on printing the data accordingly.

Post Order Traversal

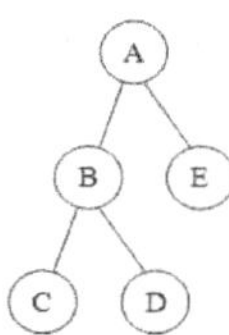

C-D-B-E-A is the post order traversal of the above figure. In the post order traversal we are following the LRD principle i.e. move to the left most node check if right sub-tree is there or not if not then print the leftmost node, if right sub-tree is there move towards the rightmost node. The key idea here is that at each sub-tree we are following the LRD principle and print the data accordingly.

Simple Binary Tree

When the data will be entered by the user, the first element will form the root node. For all the next elements user has to enter whether that element has to be inserted as aleft child or a right child of previous node. For the sake of understanding, let us build the simple binary tree for some elements.

Let us 10, now root will be formed for 10.

If next element is say 13 then user will be asked for his choice i.e. he will be asked if 13 is attached to the left or right of 10. if user answer is L (that means left) then tree will be

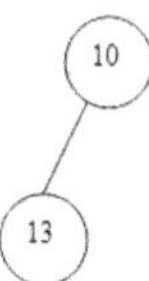

Then if the next element is 8 then again user has to give his choice, whether it is L(left) or R(right). That means first whether user want to attach 8 left or right of 10 will be asked, if user answers L then again "whether user want to attach 8 to left or right of 13 will be asked, if he answers R then, the node 8 will be attached as a right child of 13.

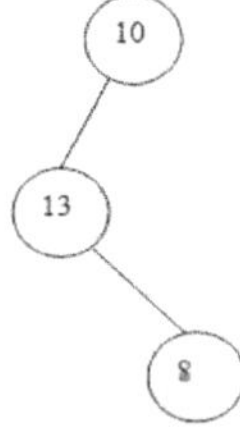

If the next element is 17 and user want to attach it as a right child of 10 then

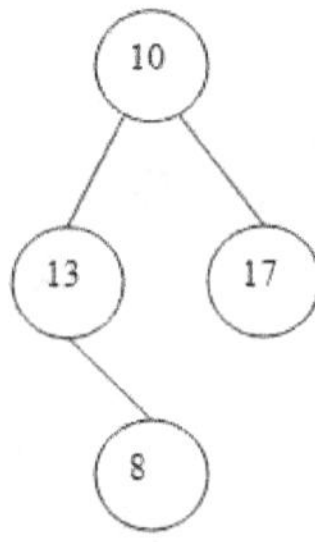

Thus a simple binary tree will be generated. The principle idea behind this creation is always ask the user where he wants to attach the next node and always start scanning the tree root.

Binary Search Tree

In the simple binary tree the nodes are arranged in any fashion. Depending on user's desire the new nodes can be attached as a left child or right child of any desired node. In such a case finding for any node is a long cut procedure, because in that case we have to search the entire tree. And thus the searching time complexity will get increased unnecessarily. So to make the searching algorithm faster in a binary tree we will go for building the binary search tree. The binary search tree is based on the binary search algorithm. While creating the binary search tree the data is systematically arranged. That means values at left sub tree < root node value < right sub tree values.

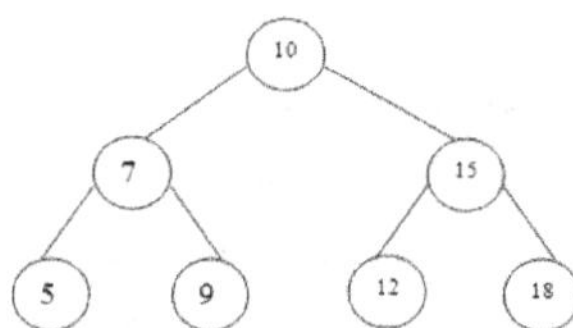

Construction of Binary Search Tree

Let us take some elements and construct a binary search tree from it.

Step 1

10	7	15	9	5	12	18

Store all the elements in an Array

Step 2

 Root node

Read the first element from the array and form the first node of the tree. Call it as root node.

Step 3

Read next element i.e. 7. As 7< 10 attach 7 as left child of 10.

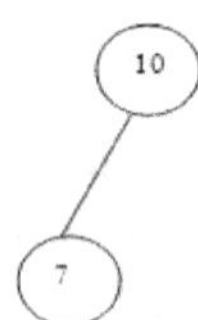

Step 4

Read next element i.e. 15. As 15 > 10 attach 15 as right child of 10

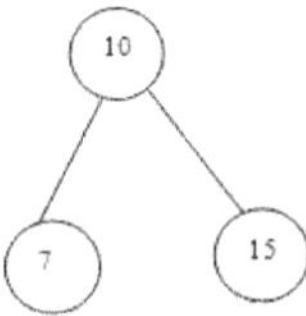

Step 5

Read next element i.e. 9. As 9 < 10 we can attach 9 as left child of 10 but already 7 is attached as left child of 10 so we will again compare 7 and 9. 9 > 7 hence 9 will be attached as right child of 7.

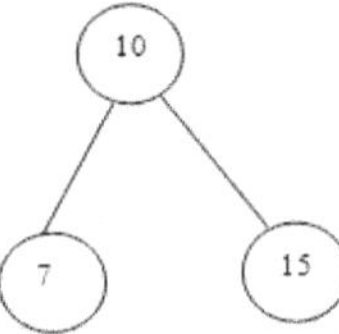

Step 6

Read next element as 5. 5 < 10 and 5 is <7. Hence 5 will be attached as a left child of 7.

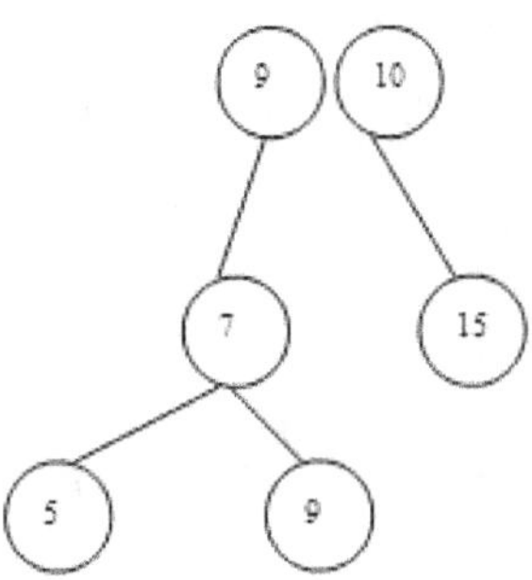

Step 7

read the next element i.e. 12. Now 12 will be compared with 10. Since 12 > 10 we can attach 12 as a right child of 10. Then we will compare 12 with 15, then 12 < 15 hence 12 will be attached as left child of 15.

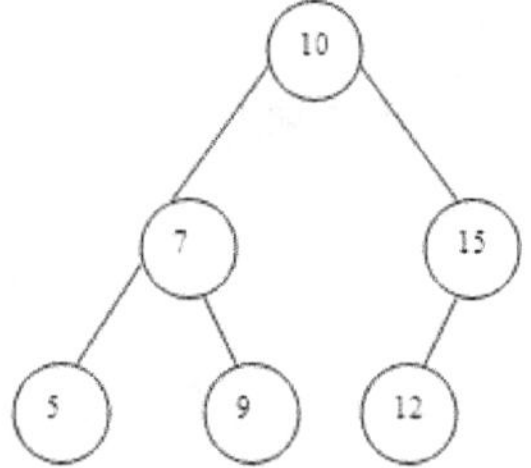

Step 8

Read the next element i.e. 18. As 18 is >10 and 15, we can attach it as right child of 15.

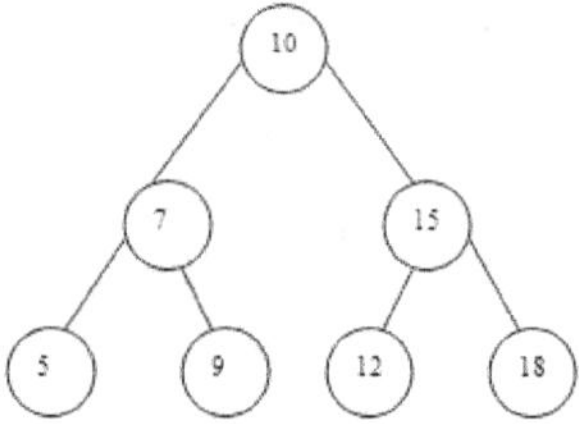

Now there is no further element in the array. Hence we will display the final binary search tree as in step 8.

If you observe the figure carefully, you will find that the left value < parent value < right value is followed throughout the tree.

Searching a Node from Binary Search Tree

Let us consider that we have already created a binary search tree as follows.

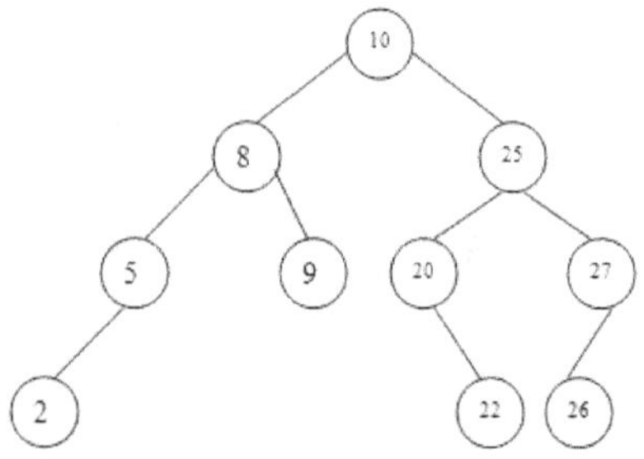

Now we want to search a node 22, from it. Then to search this desired element we will start scanning the tree from root node. Let us call the node element which we want to search as key. I.e.. Key =22. We will proceed in this way.

Step 1

Is 22>10. Then move on the right sub branch of tree from current node.

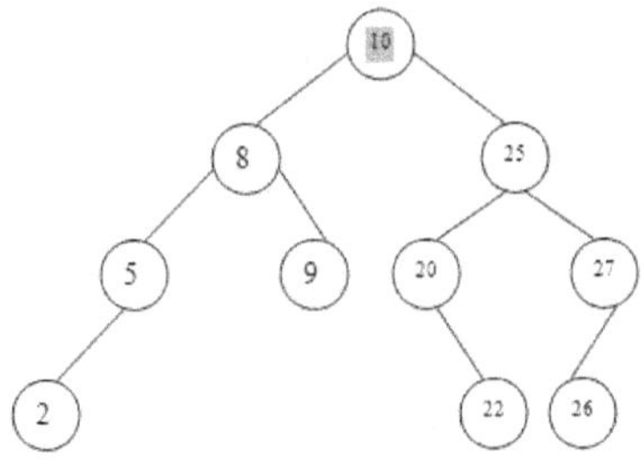

Step 2

Is 22<25. Then move the left sub branch of the tree from current node.

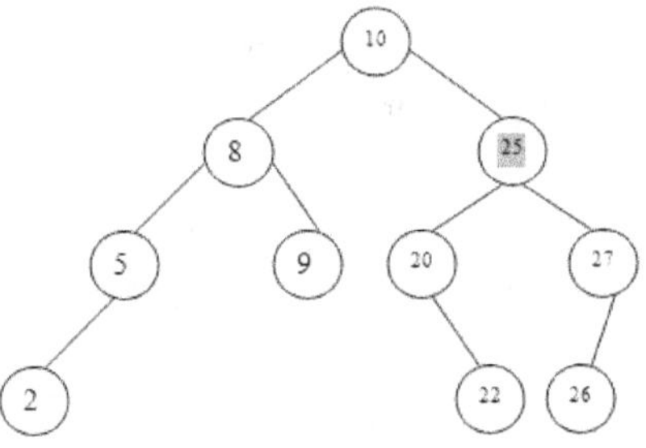

Step 3

Is 22 > 20 then move on the right sub branch of the tree from the current node.

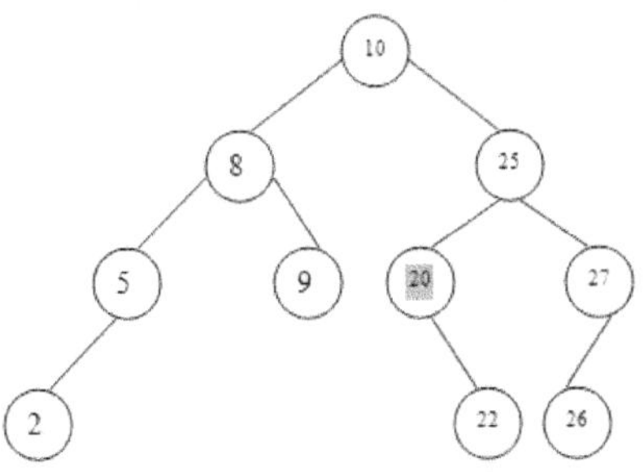

Step 4

Is 22 == 22 yes!. Match is found. Hence print the message "node 22 is present".

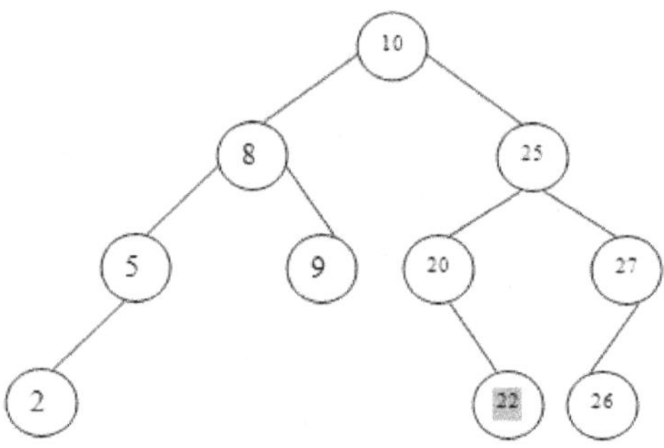

Deletion of a Node from Binary Search Tree

There are three cases for deletion of any node from binary tree. The case are as follows

Case 1: When a node which we want to delete has no child

Case 2: When a node which we want to delete has only one child(maybe left or right child)

Case 3: When a node which we want to delete has two children

With these cases we can delete any node from binary search tree. Let us discuss each case in detail.

Discussion on Case 1

The given figure shows a binary search tree. we want to delete a node 8 which has no child. This is the simplest deletion. Make the that node as NULL. Temp = NULL

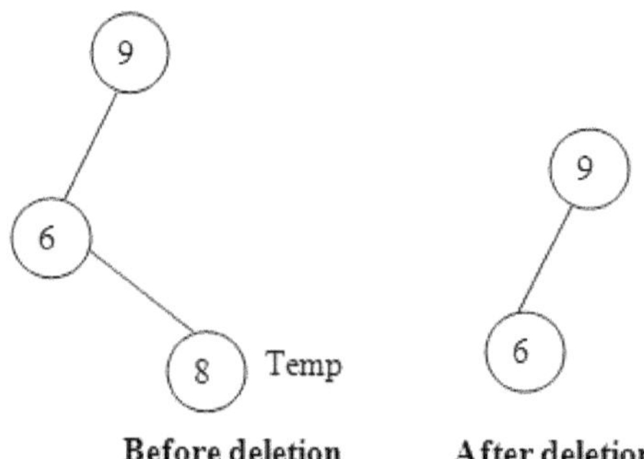

Before deletion   **After deletion**

Discussion of Case 2

When we want to delete such a node which has one child as given in figure.

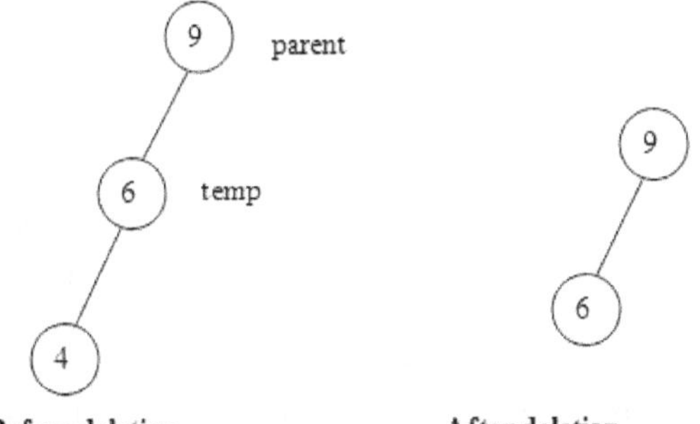

The child of 'temp' node (node to be deleted) will be the child of parent node.

The 'C' statements can be

Parent -> left = temp -> left

Free(temp);

Or it could be as follows

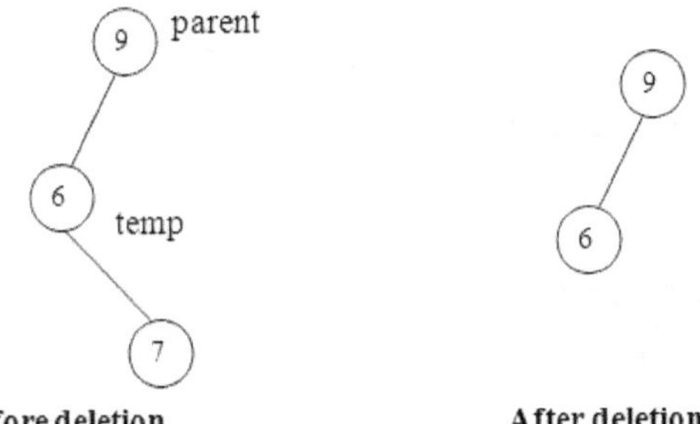

The 'C' statements can be

Parent -> left = temp -> right

Free(temp);

Discussion of Case 3

when we want to delete such a node which has two children. The figure given below show it.

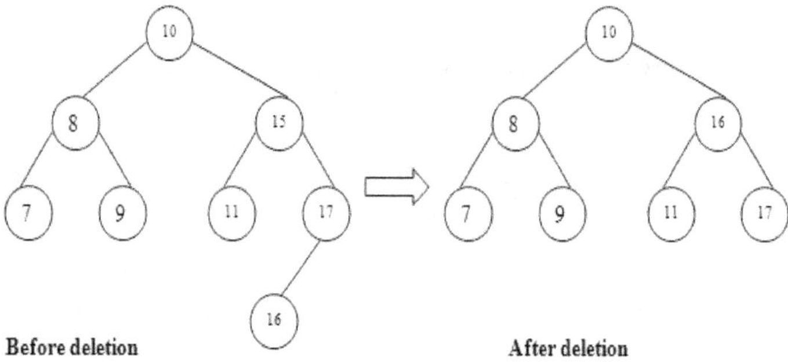

Before deletion   After deletion

The simplest technique in this type of deletion is first find the in-order successor of the node which you want to delete. Copy the value of that successor to that place. That means we want to delete the node 15 its in-order successor is 16. Hence copy 16 at 15's position and then set left pointer of node 17 to NULL.

Applications of Binary Trees

There are many applications of binary tree. For example, whenever we want to take the two-way decisions. Binary tree are the best option. One such application is a binary search tree, which we have already discussed. Binary tree can also be used to represent expressions.

Representing Expressions in Binary Trees

The arithmetic expressions represented as binary tree are know as expression trees. The root node is operator and the left and right children are operands. In case of unary operators the left child is absent and the right child is the operand. Since there is no operator available for exponent in C, the operator $ is used to denote exponent. For example the below figure shows a tree for the expression

A * B + C * D + E

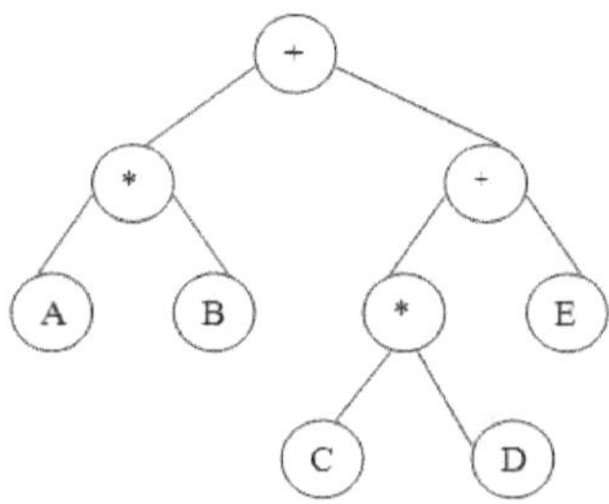

When the expression tree is traversed in pre-order then the pre-fix form of the expression is obtained. Similarly, when the expression tree is traversed in post-order then the post-fix form of the expression is obtained. In the same way we get the in-fix form of the expression when the tree is traversed in-order. But the parentheses present in the original arithmetic expression cannot be obtained back from the in-order traversal of the binary tree. This is because the structure of the binary tree itself decides the order of the evaluation of the tree.

Reconstruction of a Binary Tree

If we know the sequence of nodes obtained through in-order/pre-order/post-order traversal it may not be feasible to reconstruct the binary tree. This is because two different binary tree may yield same sequence of nodes when traversed using post-order traversal. Similarly in-order or pre-order traversal of different binary trees may yield the same sequence of nodes. However, we can construct a unique binary tree if the result of in-order and pre-order traversal are available. Let us understand this with the help of following set of in-order and pre-order traversal results.

In-order traversal: 4,7,2,8,5,1,6,9,3

Pre-order traversal: 1,2,4,7,5,8,3,6,9

We know that the first value in the pre-order traversal gives us the root of the binary tree. So the node with data 1 becomes the root of the binary tree. In in-order traversal, initially the left sub-tree is traversed then the root node and then the right sub-tree. So the data before 1 in the in-order list (i.e. 4,7,2,8,5) forms the left sub-tree and the data after 1 in the in-order list (i.e. 6,9,3) forms the right sub-tree. In below figure the structure of tree is shown after separating the tree in left and right sub-trees.

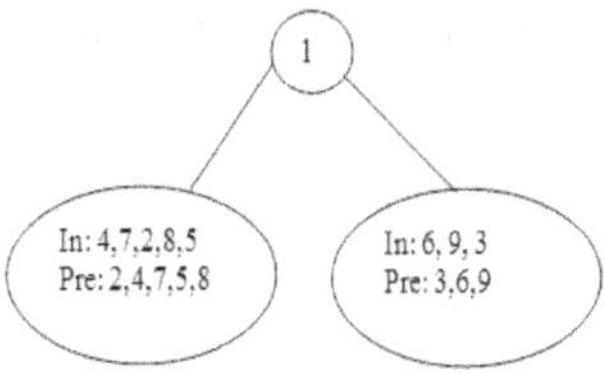

Reconstruction of Binary Tree

Now the next data in pre-order list is 2 so the root node of the left-sub-tree is 2. Hence the data before 2 in the in-order list is (i.e. 4,7) forms the left-sub-tree of the node that contains a value 2. The data that comes to the right of 2 in the in-order list (i.e. 8,5) forms the right sub-tree of the node with value 2. Below figure shows structure of tree after expanding the left and right sub-tree of the node that contains a value 2.

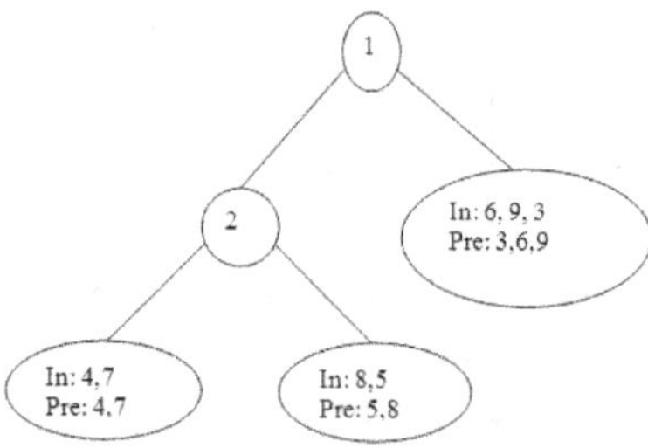

Now the next data in pre-order list is 4, so the root node of the left sub-tree of the node that contains a value 2 is 4. The data before 4 in the in-order list forms the left sub-tree of the node that contains a value 4. But as the there is no data present before 4 in in-order list, the left sub-tree of the node with value 4 is empty. The data that comes to the right of 4 in the in-order list (i.e. 7) forms the right sub-tree of the node that contains a value 4. Below figure shows structure of tree after expanding the left and right sub-tree of the node that contains a value 4.

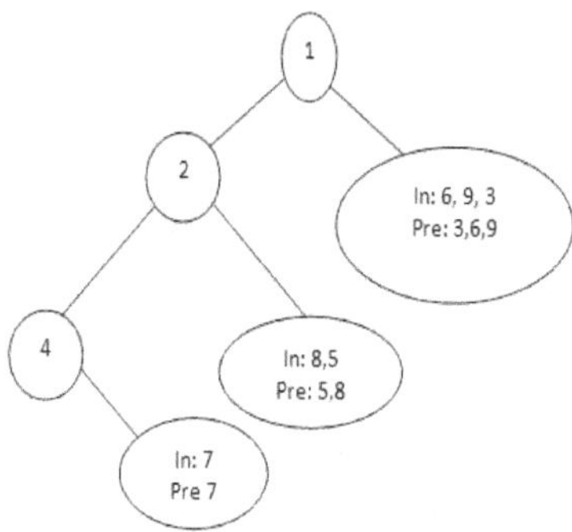

Since we are left with only one value 7 in both the pre-order and in in-order form we simply represent it with a node as shown in below figure.

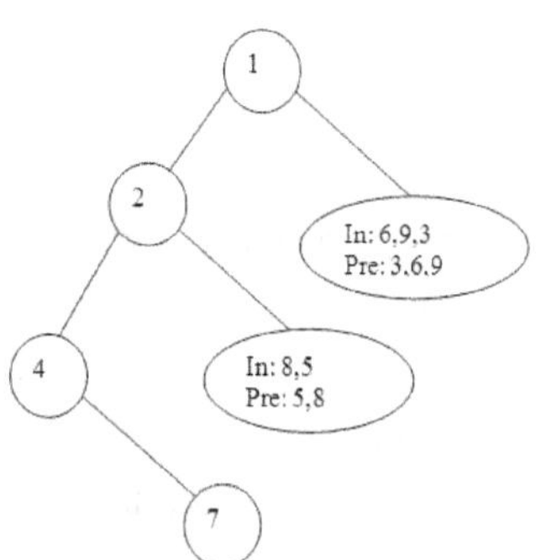

In the same way one by one all the data are picked from the pre-order list and are placed and their respective sub-trees are constructed. As a result, the whole tree is constructed.

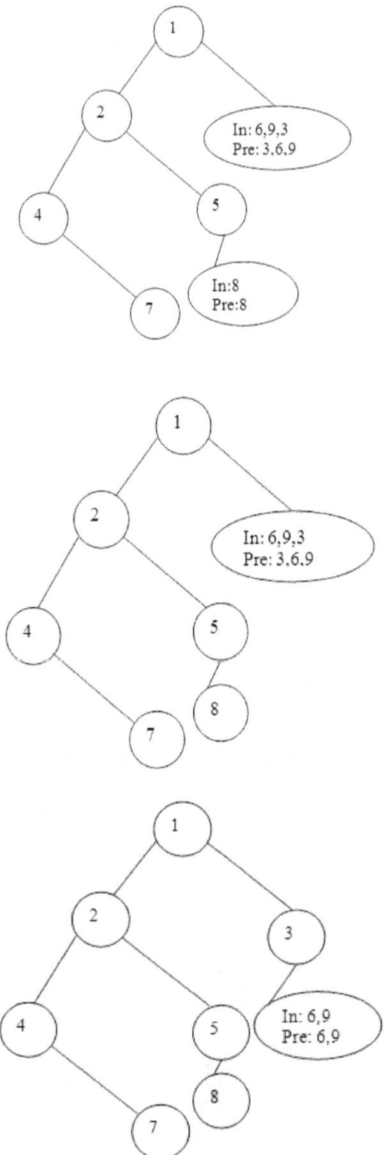

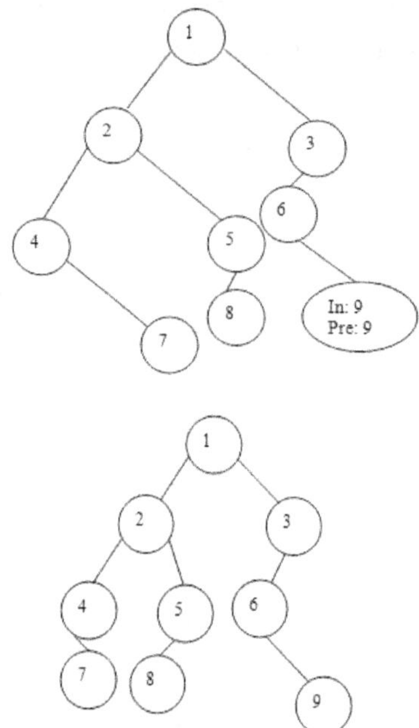

AVL Trees

An **AVL tree** is another balanced binary search tree. Named after their inventors, **Adelson-Velskii** and **Landis**, they were the first dynamically balanced trees to be proposed. Like red-black trees, they are not perfectly balanced, but pairs of sub-trees differ in height by at most 1, maintaining an *O(logn)* search time. Addition and deletion operations also take *O(logn)* time.

Definition of an AVL Tree

An AVL tree is a binary search tree which has the following properties:

1) The sub-trees of every node differ in height by at most one.
2) Every sub-tree is an AVL tree.

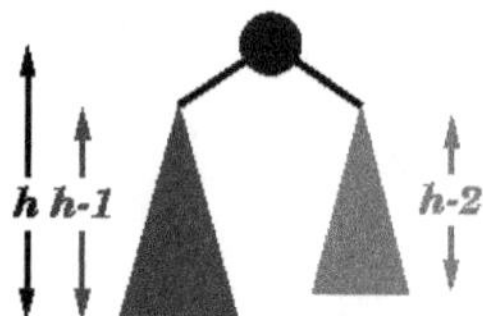

Balance requirement for an AVL tree: the left and right sub-trees differ by at most 1 in height.

You need to be careful with this definition: it permits some apparently unbalanced trees! For example, here are some trees:

Tree	**AVL Tree?**

Yes

Examination shows that each left sub-tree has a height 1 greater than each right sub-tree.

Tree	**AVL Tree?**

No

Sub-tree with root 8 has height 4 and sub-tree with root 18 has height 2.

Insertion

As with the red-black tree, insertion is somewhat complex and involves a number of cases. Implementations of AVL tree insertion may be found in many textbooks: they rely on adding an extra attribute, the **balance factor** to each node. This factor indicates whether the tree is *left-heavy* (the height of the left sub-tree is 1 greater than the right sub-tree), *balanced* (both sub-trees are the same height) or right-*heavy* (the height of the right sub-tree is 1 greater than the left sub-tree). If the balance would be destroyed by an insertion, a rotation is performed to correct the balance.

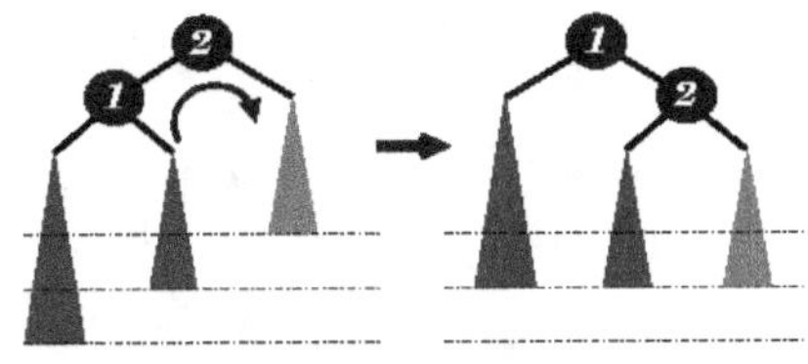

A new item has been added to the left sub-tree of node 1, causing its height to become 2 greater than 2's right sub-tree (shown in green). A right-rotation is performed to correct the imbalance.

Hashing

Hashing is an effective way to reduce the number of comparisons. Actually hashing deals with the idea of proving the direct address of the record is likely to store. To understand the idea clearly let take an example

	Key	Record
0		
1		
2	8421002	
3		
395	4618396	
396	4957397	
397		
398	1286399	
996	4618996	
997	4967997	
998	1200992	
999	0001999	

Hashing

Suppose the manufacturing company has an inventory file that consist of less than 1000 parts.

Each part is having unique 7 digit number. The number is called "key" and the particular keyed record consist of that part name. If there are less than 1000 parts then a 1000 element array can be used to store the complete file. Such an array will be indexed from 0 to 999. since the key number is 7 digit it is converted to 3 digits by taking only last 3digits of a key. This is shown in the fig.

Observe in fig that the first key 496700 and it is stored at 0th position. The second key is 8421002. The last three digits indicate the position 2nd in the array. Let us search the element 4957397.Naturally it will be obtain at position 397.This method of searching is called hashing. The function that converts the key (7 digit) into array position is called hash function.

Here hash function is

$$H(key)=key \% 1000$$

Where key % 1000 will be the hash function and the key obtained by hash function is called hash key.

Collision

From our above discussion, you might be understanding that what I mean by hash function is that function which simply takes some key value, performs some computation on it and gives as the key which is actually the address where the desired record is placed. Thus this function helps us in getting the direct access to the record. Such function is that it should not return the same key address for two different record. The situation in which the hash function returns the same address (same hash keys) for two different records is called the collision. Remember occurrence of collision means design of hash function is poor.

Any way still there are effective ways by which one can resolve the collision which are known as collision handling technique. Let us discuss those.

Collision Handling Techniques

Linear Probing

When collision occurs i.e. when two records demand for the same location in the hash table, then the collision can be solved by placing second record linearly down wherever the empty location is found.

For example

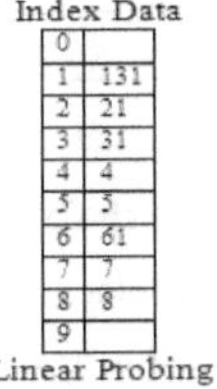

Linear Probing

In the hash table given in fig the hash function used in number % 10. if the first number which is to be placed is 131 then 131 %10= 1. i.e. remainder is 1 so hash key =1. That means we

Are supposed to place the record at index 1.

Next number is 21 which gives hash key =1 as 21 % 10 =1. But already 131 is placed at index 1.

That means collision is occurred. We will now apply linear probing. In this method, we will search the place for number 21 from location of 131. In this case we can place 21 at index 2. Then 31 at index 3. Similarly 61 can be stored at 6 because 4 and 5 are stored before 61. Because of this technique, the searching becomes efficient, as we have to search only limited list to obtain the desired number.

Chaining Without Replacement

In collision handling method changing is a concept which introduces an additional field with data i.e. chain. A separate chain table is maintained for colliding data. When collision occurs we store the second colliding data by linear probing method. The address of this colliding data can be stored with the first colliding element in the chain table, without replacement.

For example consider elements

131, 3, 4, 21, 61, 6, 71, 8, 9

Index	Data	Chain
0	-1	-1
1	-13	2
2	21	5
3	3	-1
4	4	-1
5	61	7
6	6	-1
7	71	-1
8	8	-1
9	9	-1

From the example, you can see that the chain is maintained the number who demands for location 1. First number 131 comes we will place at index 1. Next comes 21 but collision occurs so by linear probing we will place 21 at index 2, and chain is maintained by writing 2 in chain table at index 1 similarly next comes 61 by linear probing we can place 61 at index 5 and chain will be stored by linear probing at empty location but a chain is maintained so that traversing the hash table will be efficient.

The drawback of this method is in finding the next empty location. We are least bothered about the fact when the element which actually belonging to that empty location cannot obtain its location. This means logic of hash function gets distributed.

Chaining with Replacement

As previous has a drawback of loosing the meaning of the hash function, to over come this drawback the method known as changing with replacement is introduced. Let us discuss the example to understand the method. Suppose we have to store following elements: 131, 21, 31, 4, 5.

Index	Data	Chain
0	-1	-1
1	131	2
2	21	3
3	31	-1
4	4	-1
5	5	-1
6		
7		
8		
9		

Now next elements is 2. As a hash function will indicate hash key as 2 but already at index 2. We have stored element 21. But we also know that 21 is not of that position at which currently it is placed.

Hence we will replace 21 by 2 and accordingly chain table will be updated.

Index	Data	Chain
0	-1	-1
1	131	6
2	2	-1
3	31	-1
4	4	-1
5	5	-1
6	21	3
7	-1	-1
8	-1	-1
9	-1	-1

The value –1 in the hash table and chain table indicate the empty location.

The advantage of this method is that the meaning of hash function is preserved.

But each time some logic is needed to test the element, whether it is at its proper position.

Unit IV

Sorting

Sorting means arranging a set of data in some order. There are different methods that are used to sort the data in ascending or descending order. These methods can be divided into two types internal sorting and external sorting.

The internal sorting is a sorting in which the resides in the main memory of the computer. For many applications it is not possible to store the entire data on the main memory for two reasons, amount of main memory available is smaller than amount of data. Secondly the main memory is a volatile device and thus will lose the data when the power is shut down. To overcome these problems the data is stored on the secondary storage devices. The technique which is used to sort the data which resides on the secondary devices are called external sorting.

Internal Sorting

Sorting is an important activity and every time we insert or delete the data we need to sort the remaining data. Therefore it should be carried out efficiently. Various algorithms are developed for sorting such as:

1) Bubble sort
2) Insertion sort
3) Shell sort
4) Heap sort
5) Merge sort
6) Quick sort

1) Bubble Sort

This is the simplest kind of sorting method in this method. We do this bubble sort procedure in several iterations, which are called passes.

Algorithm

1. Read the total number of elements says n
2. Store the elements in the array
3. Set i=0
4. Compare the adjacent elements
5. Repeat the step 4 for all n elements.

6. Increment the value of I by 1 and repeat step 4,5 for I<n

7. Print the sorted list of elements.

8. Stop

For example – consider following set of elements

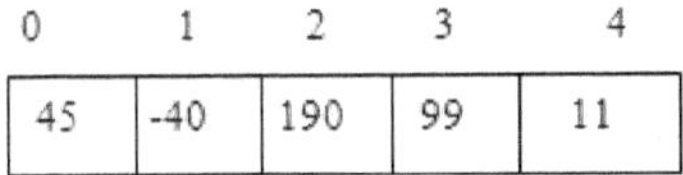

First Pass

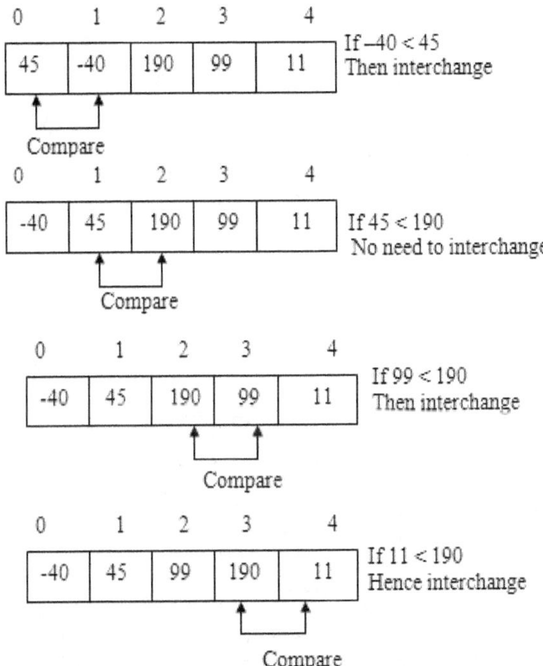

After First Pass

Now in second pass we will do comparison from 0th position to 3rd position.

Second Pass

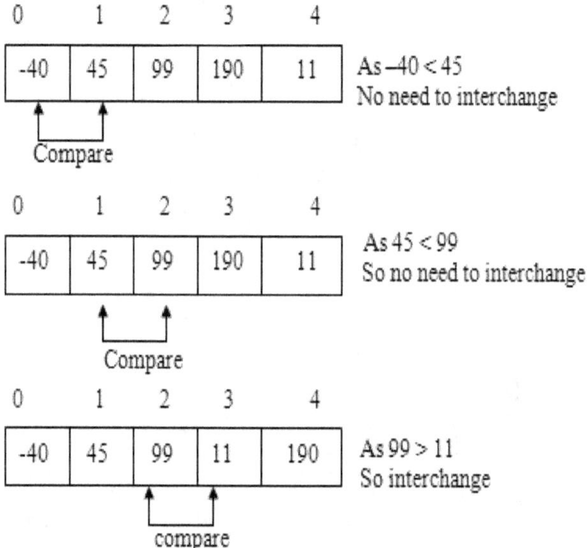

Now in third pass we will compare from 0th to 2nd location.

After Second Pass

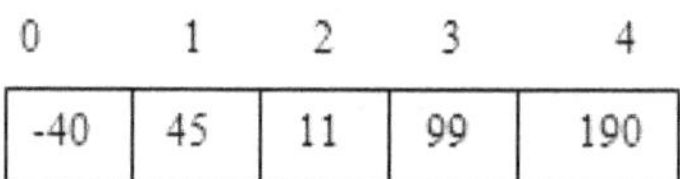

Now in third pass we will compare from 0th to 2nd location.

Third Pass

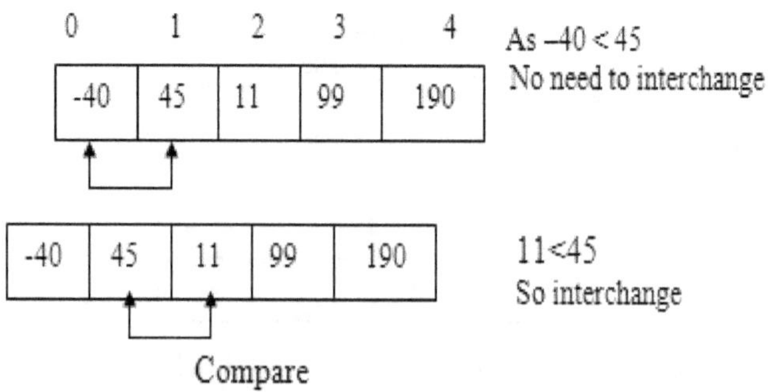

After Third Pass

	0	1	2	3	4
	-40	11	45	99	190

Now in 4th pass compare elements from 0th to 1st location.

Fourth Pass

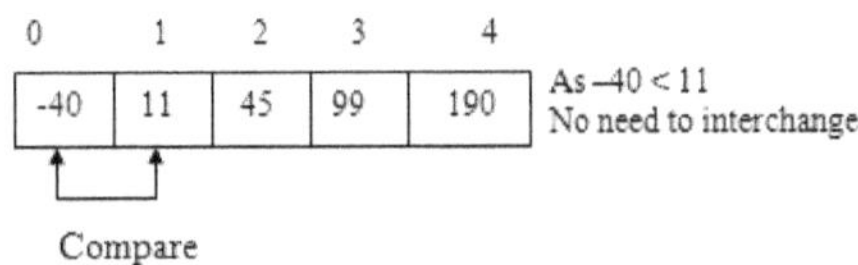

Now we will stop comparison and finally print the array which is now in sorted form

	0	1	2	3	4
	-40	11	45	99	190

This is how bubble sort works.

'C' Program

```c
/*Bubble sort. */
#include <stdio.h>
#include <conio.h>
void main( )
{
    int n,a[20];
    int i, j, temp ;
    clrscr( );
    printf("enter the limit");
    scanf("%d",&n);
    printf("enter the array values:");
    for(i=0;i<n;i++)
    {
    scanf("%d",&a[i]);
    }
    printf ( "Bubble sort.\n" ) ;
```

```c
        printf ( "\nArray before sorting:\n") ;

    for ( i = 0 ; i < n ; i++ )
            printf ( "%d\t", a[i] ) ;

    for ( i = 0 ; i < n-1 ; i++ )
    {
            for ( j = 0 ; j <n-i-1; j++ )
            {
                    if ( a[j] > a[j + 1] )
                    {
                            temp = a[j] ;
                            a[j] = a[j + 1] ;
                            a[j + 1] = temp ;
                    }
            }
    }

    printf ( "\n\nArray after sorting:\n") ;

    for ( i = 0 ; i < n ; i++ )
            printf ( "%d\t", a[i] ) ;
    getch( ) ;
}
```

Output:

enter the limit5

enter the array values:45

-40

190

99

11

Bubble sort.

Array before sorting:

45   -40   190   99   11

Array after sorting:

-40   11   45   99   190

2) Insertion Sort

In this method elements are inserted at their appropriate places. Let us see the example.
Consider an array a contains 5 elements.

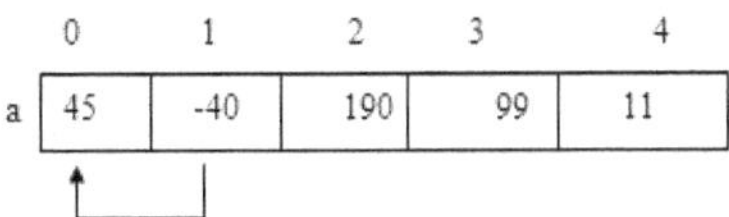

First Iteration

Compare a [1] with a [0]

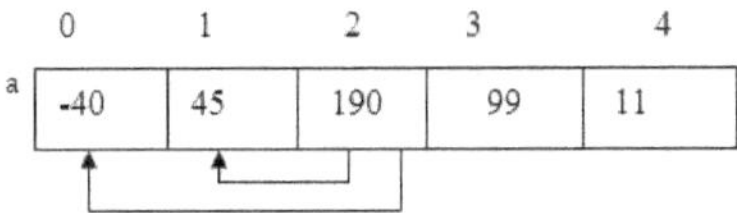

After First Iteration

Second Iteration

Compare a [2] with a[0] and a [1]

After Second Iteration

Third Iteration

Compare a[3] with a[0],a[1] and a[2].

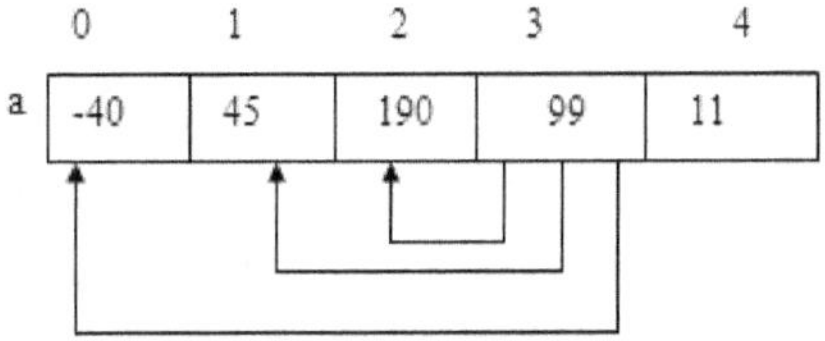

After Third Iteration

	-40	45	99	190	11

a

Fourth Iteration

Compare a[4] with a[0],a[1],a[2] and a[3].

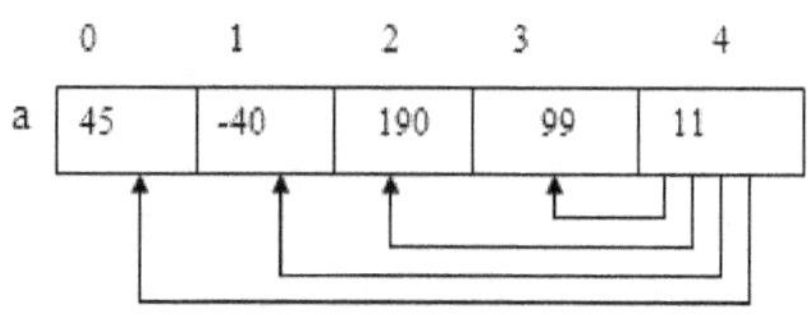

After Fourth Iteration

	0	1	2	3	4
a	-40	11	45	99	190

'C' Program

```c
/* Insertion sort. */
#include <stdio.h>
#include <conio.h>

void main( )
{
    int a[25];
    int i, j, k, temp,n ;
    clrscr( ) ;
    printf("enter the number of elements:");
    scanf("%d",&n);
    printf("enter the elements:");
    for(i=0;i<n;i++)
    {
    scanf("%d",&a[i]);
    }
    printf ( "Insertion sort.\n" ) ;
```

```c
printf ( "\nArray before sorting:\n") ;
for (i=0;i<n;i++)
printf ( "%d\t", a[i] ) ;
for ( i = 1 ; i < n ; i++ )
{
for ( j = 0 ; j < i ; j++ )
{
if ( a[j] > a[i] )
{
temp = a[j] ;
a[j] = a[i] ;
a[i]=temp ;
}
}
}
printf ( "\n\nArray after sorting:\n") ;
for ( i = 0 ; i < n ; i++ )
printf ( "%d\t", a[i] ) ;
getch( ) ;
}
```

Output:

enter the number of elements:5

enter the elements:25

17

31

13

2

Insertion sort.

Array before sorting:

25   17   31   13   2

Array after sorting:

2   13   17   25   31

3) *Shell Sort*

This method is improvement over the simple insertion sort. In this method the elements at fixed distance are compared. The distance will then be decremented by some fixed amount and again the comparison will be made. Finally, individual elements will be compared. Let us take some example.

Example

	0	1	2	3	4	5	6	7
x	25	57	48	37	12	92	86	33

Step 1: let us take the distance k = 5

so in the first iteration compare

(x [0] , x[5])

(x[1], x[6])

(x[2], x[7])

(x[3])

(x[4])

i.e.

First Iteration

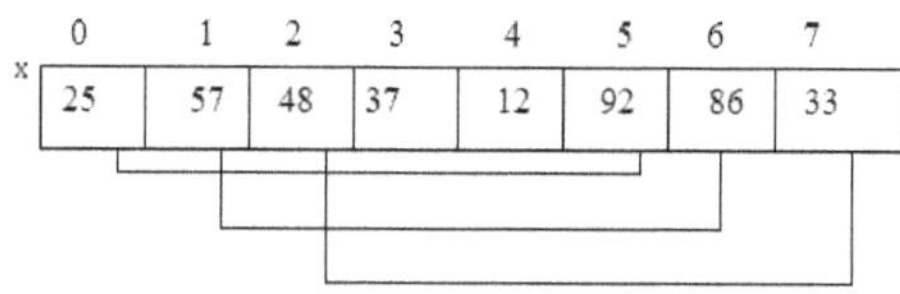

After First Iteration

	0	1	2	3	4	5	6	7
	25	57	33	37	12	92	86	48

Step 2: initially K was 5. take some d and decrement k by d. let us take d=2

∴ k= k-d i.e. k=5-2= 3

so now compare

(x[0],x[3],x[6])

(x[1],x[4],x[7])

(x[2], x[5])

Second Iteration

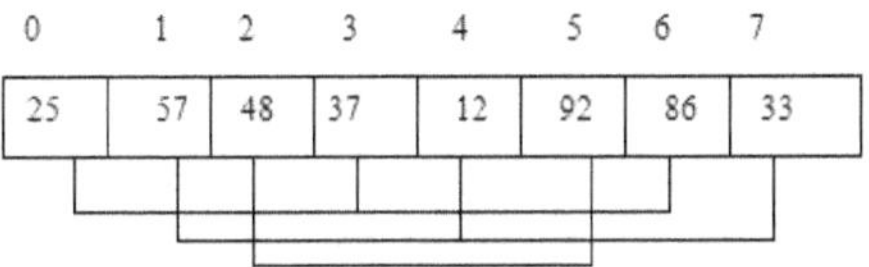

After Second Iteration

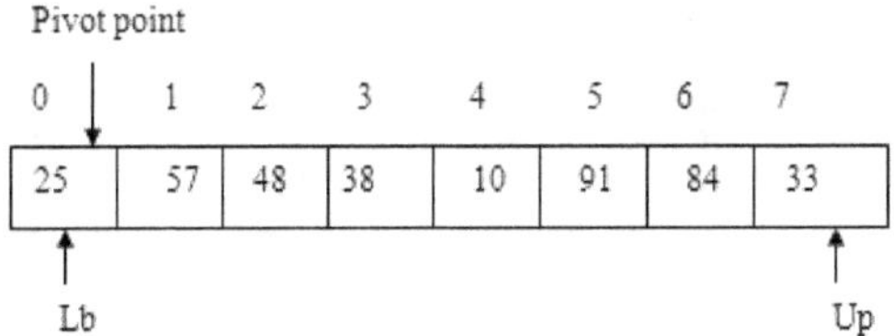

Step 3: Now k=k-d ∴ k=3-2 = 1

so now compare

(x[0], x[1], x[2], x[3], x[4], x[5], x[6], x[7])

This sorting is then done by simple insertion sort. Because simple insertion sort is highly efficient on sorted file. So we get

0	1	2	3	4	5	6	7
12	25	33	37	48	57	86	92

4) Quick Sort

This is the efficient sorting technique which is based on divide and conquer strategy.

Let us take few elements and store them in the array

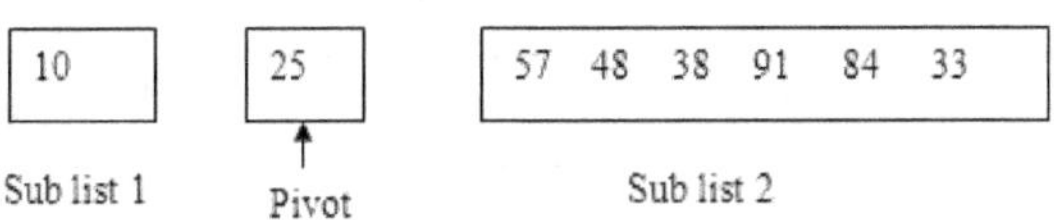

Step 1: Set the a[0]th element i.e. 25 as pivot element. The index 0 of array a is lower bound and the index 7 is the upper bound.

Now find all the elements lesser than 25 and place 25 after all the lesser elements.

Step 2: As in sub-list 1 only one element is present no need to sort it. But sub-list 2 can be sorted. For that purpose now set new pivot element as 57 find all the lesser than 57 elements and place them before 57.

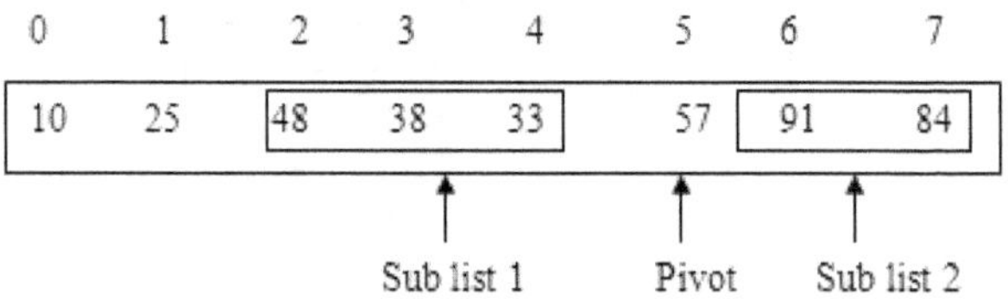

Step 3: As again from sub-list 1 and sub-list 2 sort the elements take sub-list 1, 48 is new pivot element place all lesser than 48 elements before it.

Step 4

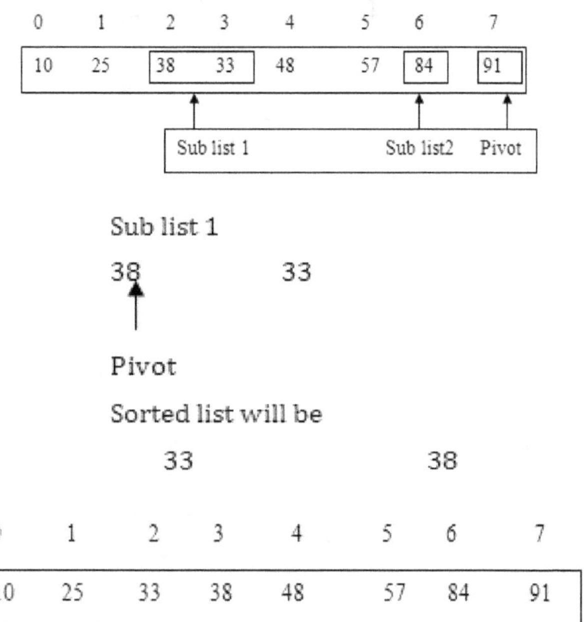

Thus the list is sorted by quick sort.

Algorithm

1. Read the total number of elements in the list say n.
2. Store the elements in the array
3. Take the first element from the array and call it as the pivot element
4. Now find all the elements which are less than this pivot element and place them before the pivot element. Thus the array will be divided in the lesser elements, pivot element and elements greater then the pivot element.
5. Repeat the step 4 each time placing the pivot element at its proper position. Thus the complete list will get sorted.

'C' Program

```c
/* Quick sort. */

#include <stdio.h>
#include <conio.h>

int split ( int*, int, int ) ;

void main( )
{
    int arr[10] = { 11, 2, 9, 13, 57, 25, 17, 1, 90, 3 } ;
    int i ;

    void quicksort ( int *, int, int ) ;

    clrscr( ) ;

    printf ( "Quick sort.\n" ) ;
    printf ( "\nArray before sorting:\n") ;

    for ( i = 0 ; i <= 9 ; i++ )
            printf ( "%d\t", arr[i] ) ;

    quicksort ( arr, 0, 9 ) ;
```

```c
		printf ( "\nArray after sorting:\n") ;

	for ( i = 0 ; i <= 9 ; i++ )
			printf ( "%d\t", arr[i] ) ;

	getch( ) ;
}


void quicksort ( int a[ ], int lower, int upper )
{
	int i ;
	if ( upper > lower )
	{
			i = split ( a, lower, upper ) ;
			quicksort ( a, lower, i - 1 ) ;
			quicksort ( a, i + 1, upper ) ;
	}
}


int split ( int a[ ], int lower, int upper )
{
	int i, p, q, t ;

	p = lower + 1 ;
	q = upper ;
	i = a[lower] ;

	while ( q >= p )
	{
			while ( a[p] < i )
					p++ ;

			while ( a[q] > i )
					q-- ;
```

```
            if ( q > p )
            {
                    t = a[p] ;
                    a[p] = a[q] ;
                    a[q] = t ;
            }
    }
    t = a[lower] ;
    a[lower] = a[q] ;
    a[q] = t ;
    return q ;
}
```

Output:

Quick sort.

Array before sorting:

11   2   9   13   57   25   17   1   90   3

Array after sorting:

1   2   3   9   11   13   17   25   57   90

5) Heap Sort

Heap sort is a method in which a binary tree is used. In this method first the heap is created using binary tree and then heap is sorted using priority queue.

Example for Heap Sort

In the heap sort method we will first take all the elements in the array a

	0	1	2	3	4	5	6	7
a	25	57	48	38	10	91	84	33

Now start building the heap structure. In forming the heap the key point is build heap in such a way that the highest value in the array will always be a root.

Step 1

Step 2

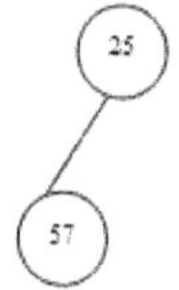

Step 3

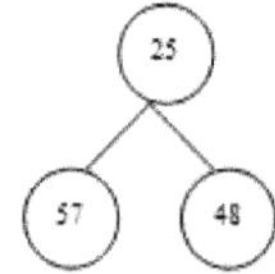

Step 4

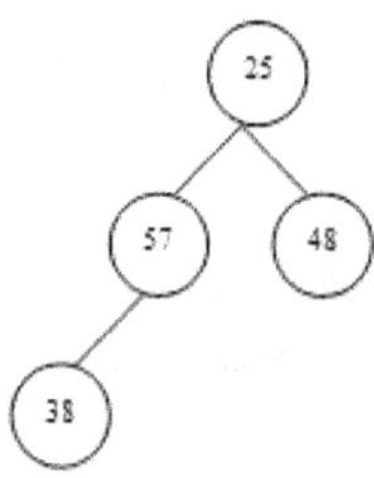

Step 5

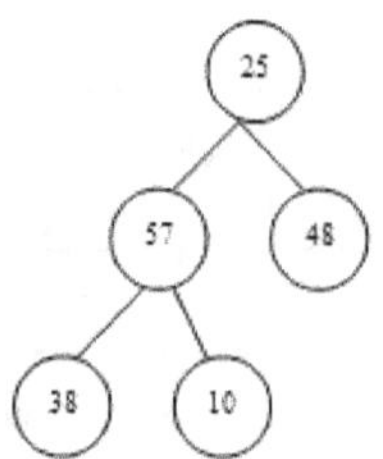

Step 6

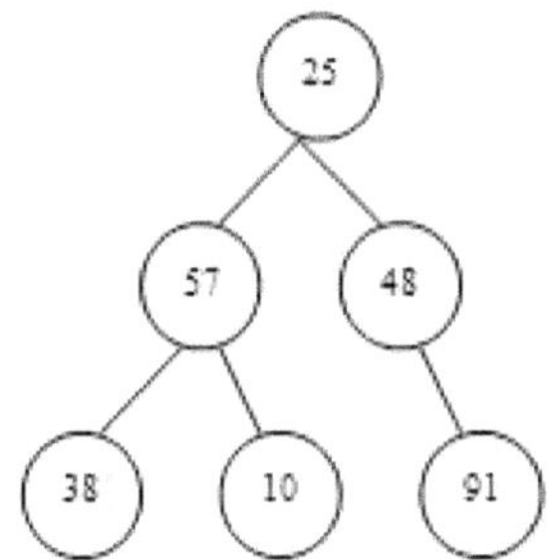

Step 7

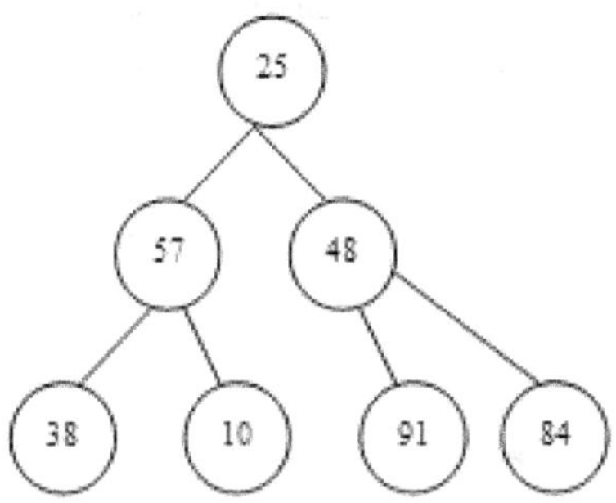

Step 8

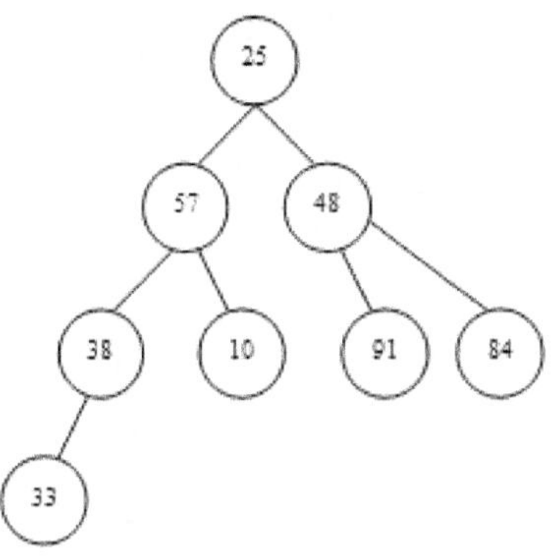

Step 9

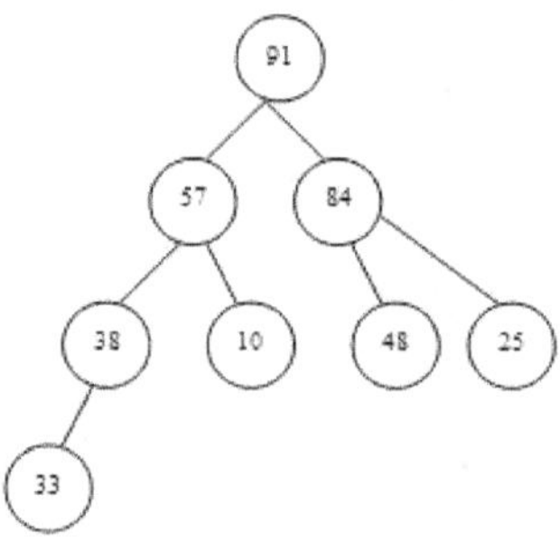

Now the heap is formed. Let us sort it. For sorting the heap remember two main things the first thing is that the binary tree form of the heap should not be disturbed at all. For the complete sorting binary tree should be remained. And the second thing is that we will start storing the higher elements at the end of array in sorted manner i.e. a[7] = 91, a[6]=84 and so on.

Step 1

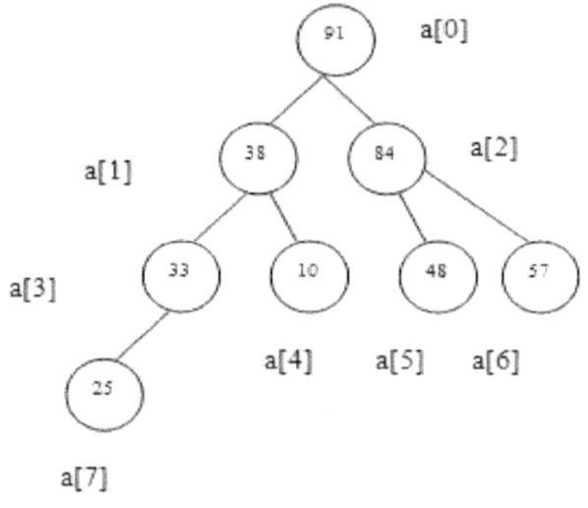

Remove 91 from a[0] and place it at a[7]

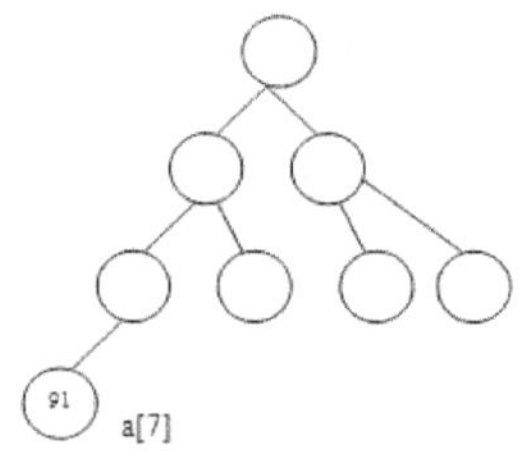

Now its 84 nodes turn, so make it root and adjust the other nodes accordingly.

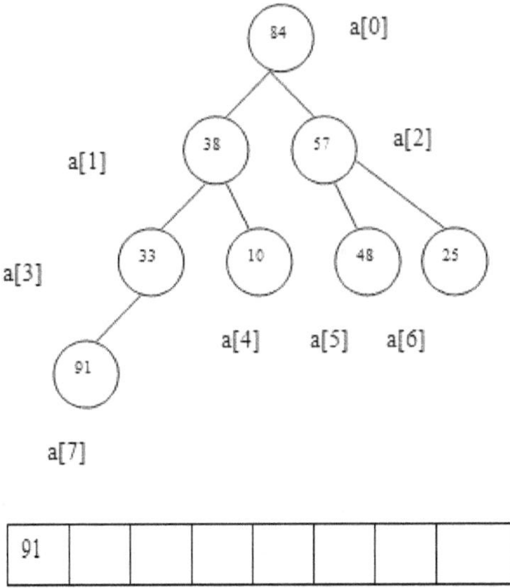

The sorted array can be maintained, we call it a queue in which a[7] element can be inserted.

Step 2

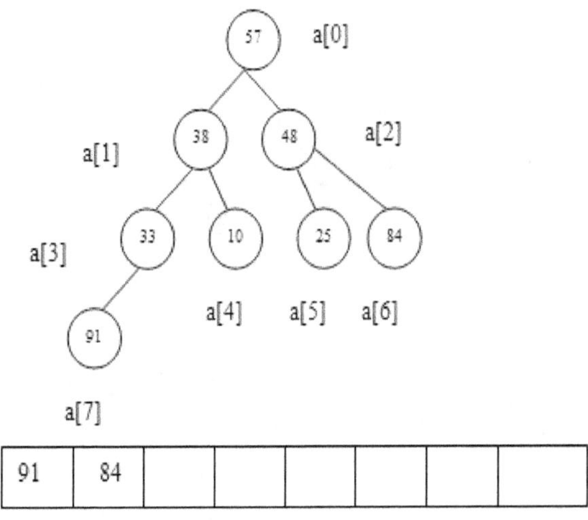

Step 3

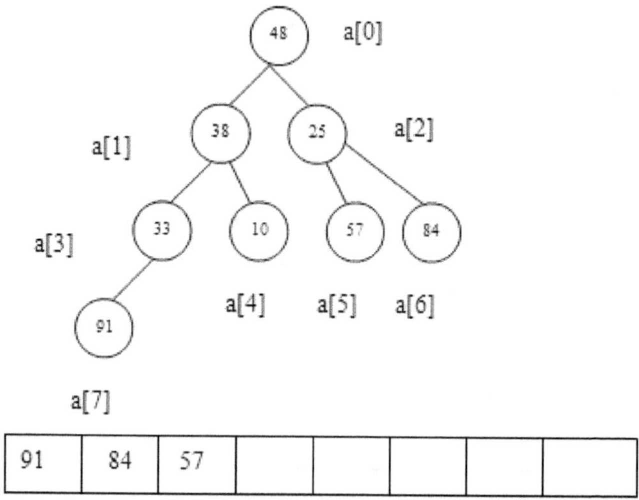

91	84	57					

Step 4

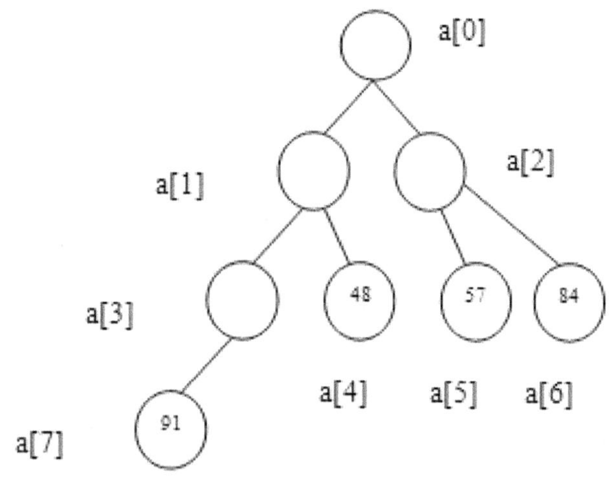

Adjust the remaining nodes. Te sorted queue will be.

91	84	57	48				

Step 5

Now next higher element is 38 so put it at root's position and adjust the remaining nodes.

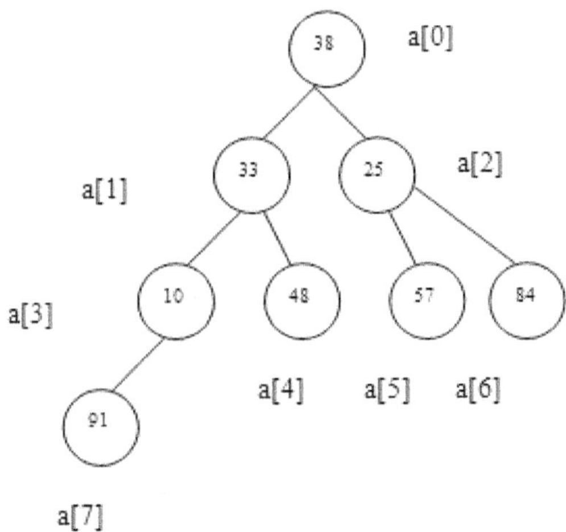

Now remove a[0] element i.e. 38 and place it at its position means at a[3]. Adjust remaining node accordingly.

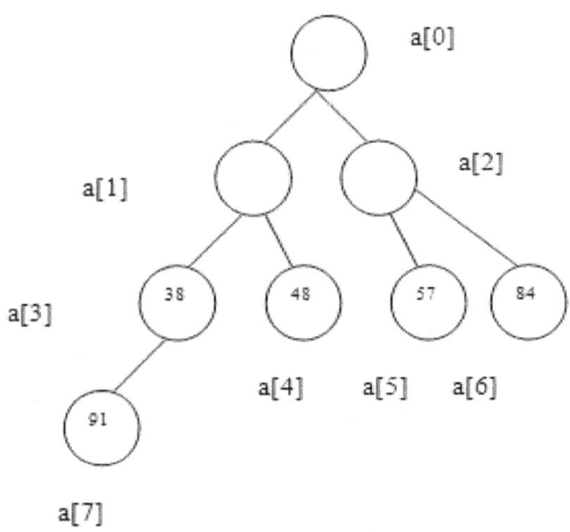

The element a[3] will be in the queue. The sorted queue will look like this

91	84	57	48	38			

Step 6

The next element is 33. So place 33 at root.

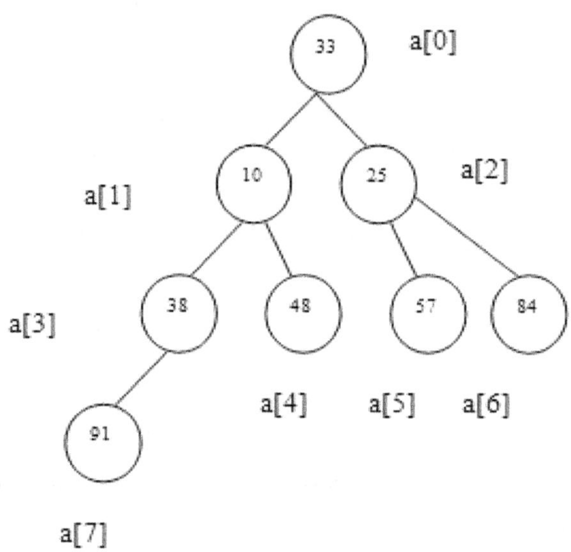

Now place a[0] at a[2] i.e. place at is position

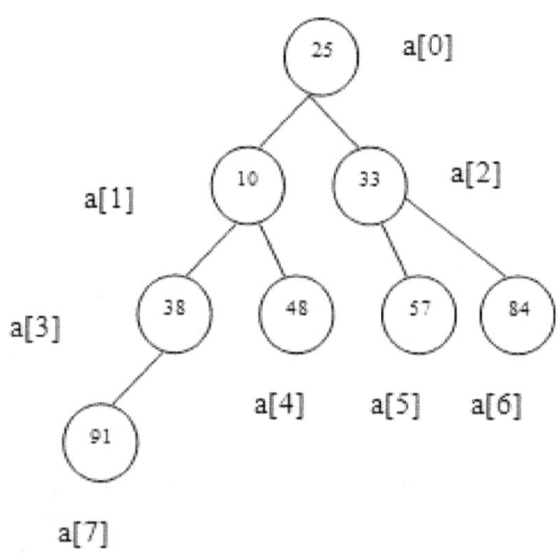

Now insert the data at a[3] i.e. 33 in the queue. So the queue will look like this

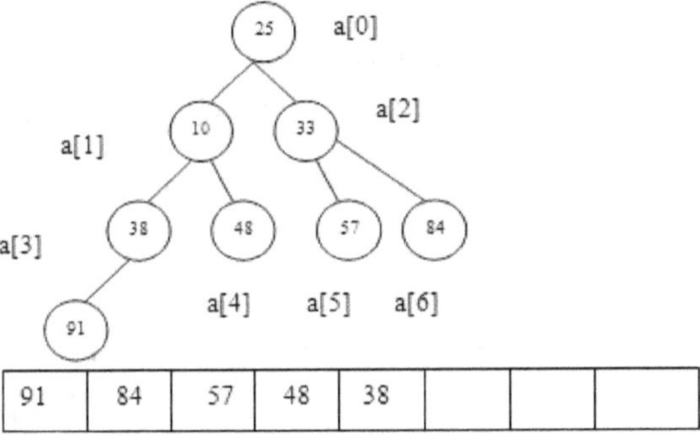

Step 7

The next higher element is 25. Place it at a[1].

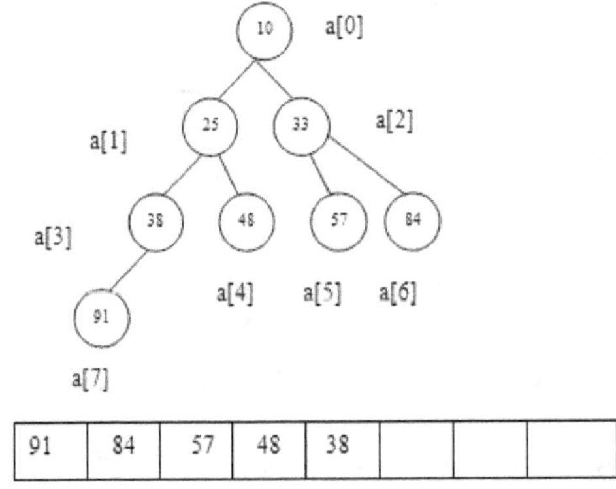

Step 8

The remaining element 10 has already occupied its proper position because only one place as empty so insert 10 also in the queue.

Queue

91	84	57	48	38	33	25	10

Front   Rear

So print the front element and then delete it. Thus in descending order the elements are sorted by heap sort method.

6) *Merge Sort*

In this sorting method, we divide the main list into two sub-lists, then go on dividing those sub-list till we get sufficient length of that sub-list. Then we compare and sort the elements of each list. Merge the two sub-list and sort the merged the list. This process will be repeated until we get only one sorted list.

For example

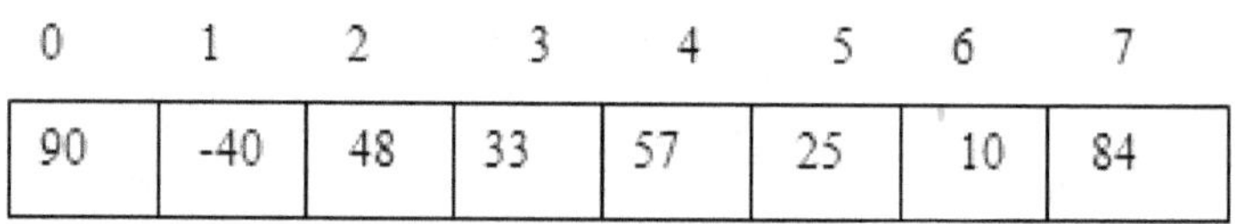

The elements are stored in an array we will go on dividing the array

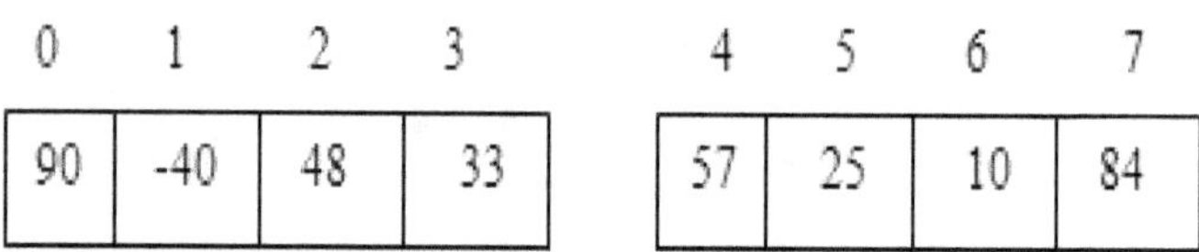

Again divide each sub-list

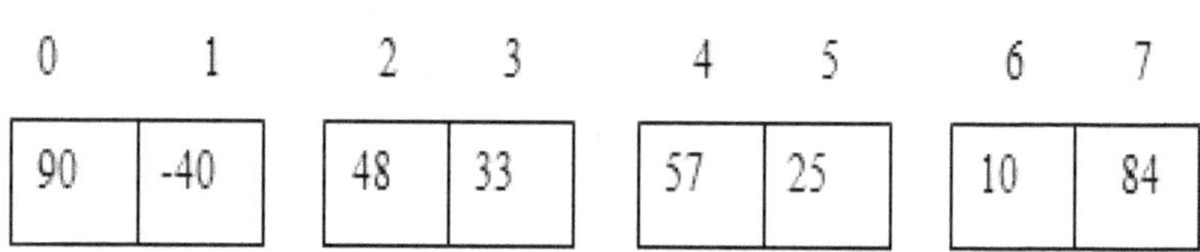

Now if we try to divide the sub-lists we will get single element in each list

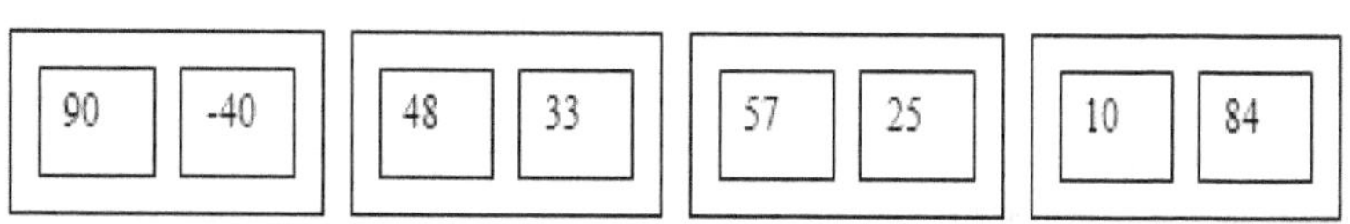

Further division is not possible. Hence we will stop dividing and start merging

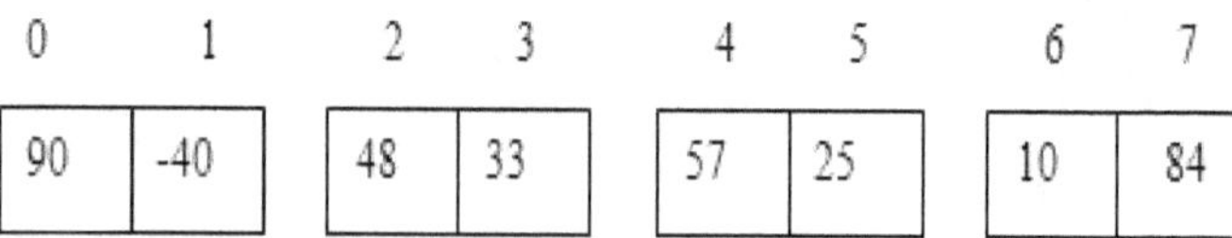

Now sort them in that sub-list only

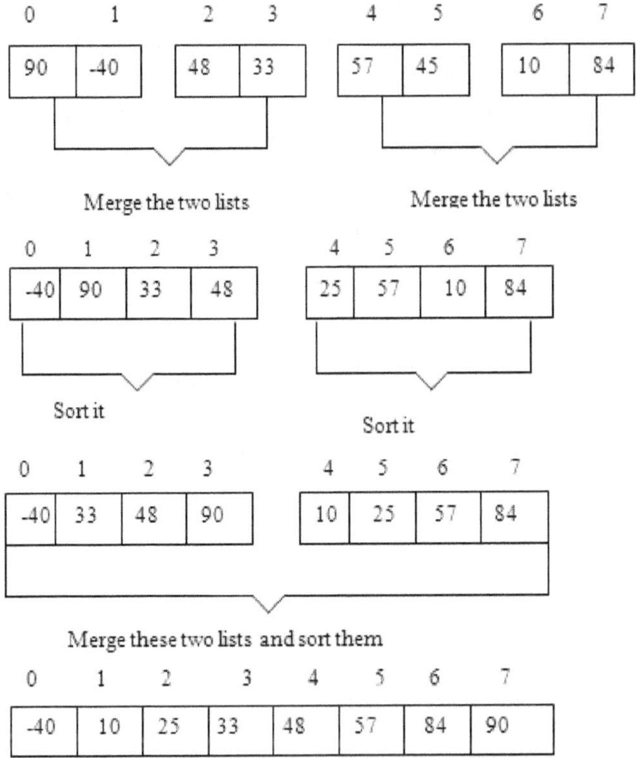

Here is a sorted list.

Analysis of All the Sorting Method

Sorting	Best case	Average case	Worst case
Bubble sort	O(n²)	O(n²)	O(n²)
Insertion Sort	O(n)	O(n²)	O(n²)
Shell Sort	O(n)	O(n²)	O(n²)
Heap Sort	O(n log n)	O(n log n)	O(n log n)
Merge Sort	O(n log n)	O(n log n)	O(n log n)
Quick Sort	O(log n)	O(log n)	O(n²)

External Sorting

External sorting is a complex sorting technique. When a large data has to be sorted and if we need to place part of data on the main memory and remaining on the secondary memory then external sorting can be done.

The data stored on secondary memory is part loaded into the main memory, sorting can be done over there. The sorted data can be then stored in the intermediate files. Thus many intermediate files can be generated. And finally all the sorted intermediate files are merged in a single file. Thus the huge amount of data can be sorted using this technique.

UNIT V

GRAPHS

Definition of Graph

A graph is a collection of two sets V and E where V is a finite non empty set of vertices and E is a finite non empty set of edges.

Vertices are nothing but the nodes in the graph and the two adjacent vertices are joined by edges. The graph is thus a set of two sets. Any graph G is denoted by G = {V,E}

Types of Graph

Basically graphs are classified in to two types

1. Directed graphs
2. Un directed graphs

In the directed graph the directions are shown on the edges. As shown in the following figure the edges between the vertices are ordered.

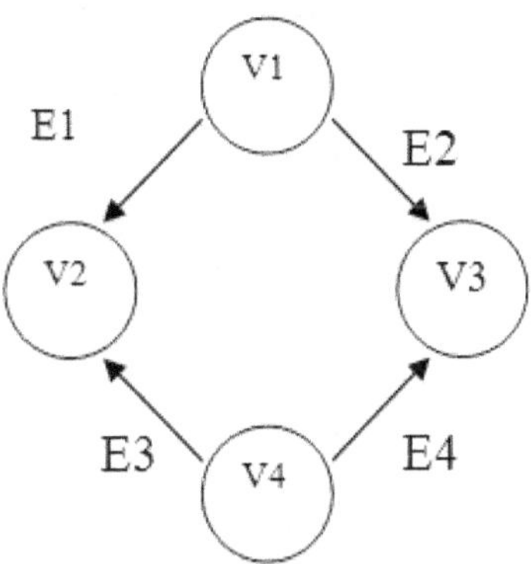

Directed Graph

In this type of graph, the edge E1 is in between vertices V1 and V2. the V1 is called head and the V2 is called the tail. Similarly for V1 head the tail is V3 and so on.

We can say E1 is the set of (V1, V2) and not of (V2,V1).

Similarly, in an undirected graph, the edges are not ordered. In this type of Graph the edge E1 is the set of (V1,V2) or (V2,V1).

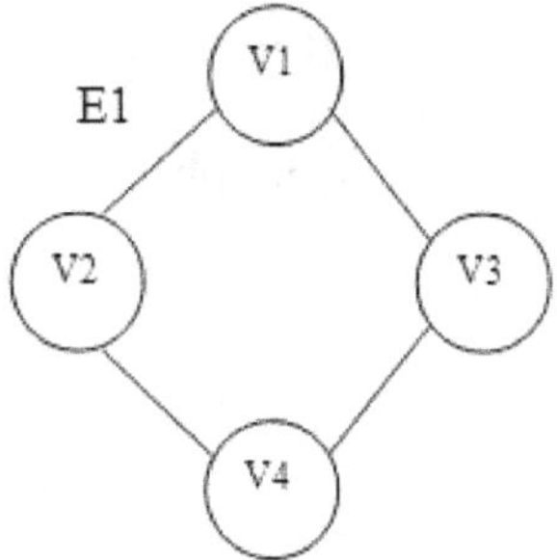

Properties of Graph

Complete Graph

If an undirected graph of n vertices consists of n(n-1)/2 number of edges then it is called as complete graph.

The graph shown in following figure is a complete graph.

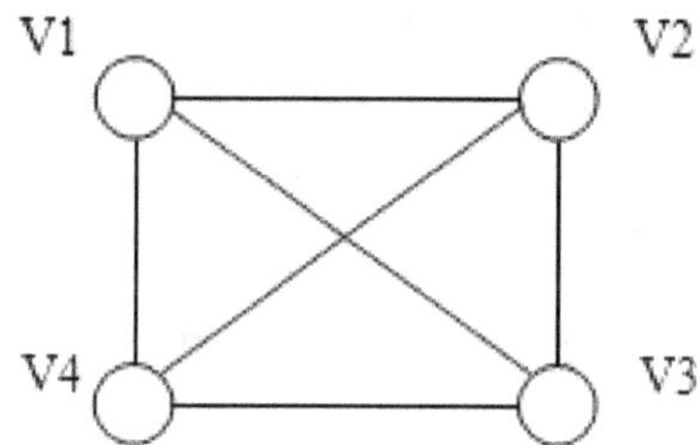

Complete Graph

Sub Graph

A sub graph G′ of graph is a graph such that the set of vertices and set of edges of G′ are proper subset of the set of edges of G.

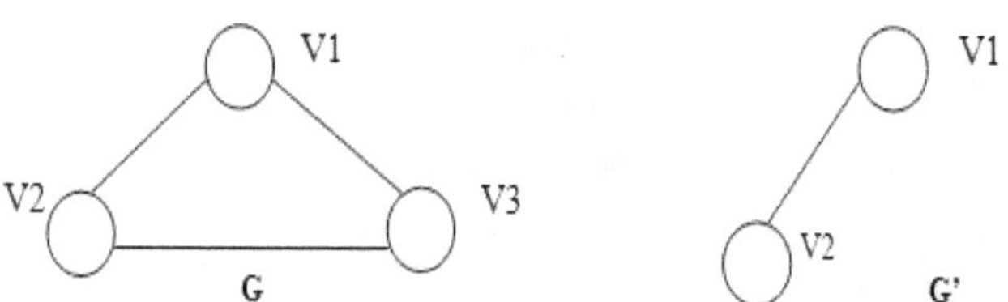

Connected Graph

An undirected graph is said to be connected if for every pair of distinct vertices Vi and Vj in V(G) there is a graph from Vi to Vj in G.

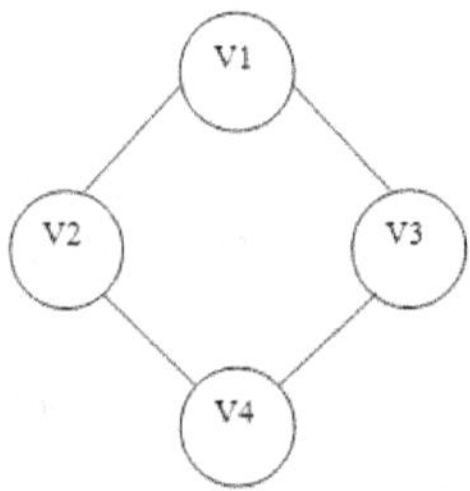

Representation of Graphs

There are several representation of graph, but we will discuss the two commonly used representations called

1) Adjacency matrix
2) Adjacency lists

Adjacency Matrix Representation

The adjacency matrix of G is a 2-dimensional array of size n*n (where n is the number of vertices in the graph). Consider a graph G of n vertices and the matrix M. if there is an edge present between vertices Vi and Vj then M[I][j]=1 else M[I][j]=0. note that for an undirected graph if M[I][j]=1 then M[j][I] is also 1. Here are some graphs shown by adjacency matrix.

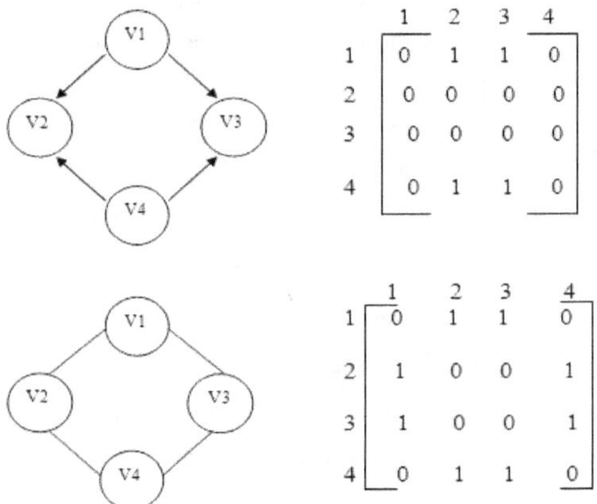

As can be seen from above, the adjacency matrix for an undirected graph is symmetric. The adjacency matrix for a directed graph need not be symmetric. The space needed to represent a graph using its adjacency matrix is n² locations. About half this space can be saved in the case of undirected graphs by storing only the upper or lower triangle of the matrix.

Adjacency Lists

In this representation the n rows of the adjacency matrix are represented as n linked lists. There is one list for each vertex in the graph. The nodes in list I represent the vertices that are adjacent from vertex i. Each list has a head node.

The head nodes are sequential providing easy random access to the adjacency list for any particular vertex. The adjacency lists for graphs G1 and G2 are shown below.

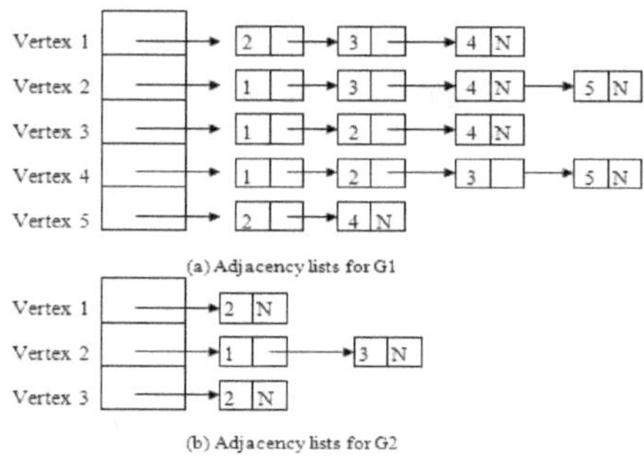

Adjacency Lists

Given the root node of a binary tree, one of the most common operations performed is visiting every node of the tree in some order. Similarly, given a vertex in a directed or undirected graph we may wish to visit all vertices in two ways_ using the Depth First Search and the Breadth First Search algorithm.

Depth First Search

The algorithm for Depth first search of an undirected graph is as follows:

1) Visit is a vertex, say v. Mark this vertex as visited.
2) Select an unvisited vertex w adjacent to v.
3) Repeat steps (a) and (b) till all adjacent vertices of w are visited.
4) On reaching a vertex adjacent to it and go back to step (a).
5) Terminate the search when no unvisited vertex can be reached from any of the visited ones.

Explanation of Logic for Depth First Traversal

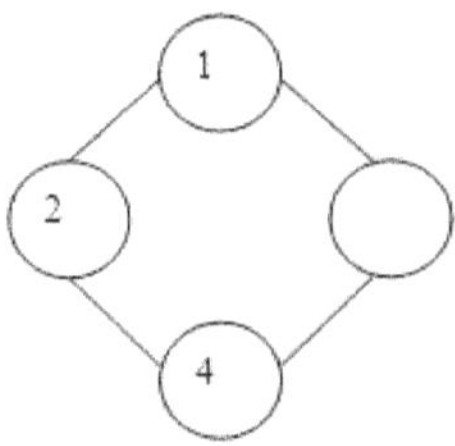

In DFS the basic data structure for storing the adjacent nodes is stack. In the algorithm we have used a recursive call to DFS function. When a recursive call is invoked actually push operations get performed. When we exit form the loop pop operation will be performed. Let us see how our algorithm works.

Step 1: start with vertex 1, print it. So '1' gets printed. Mark 1 as visited.

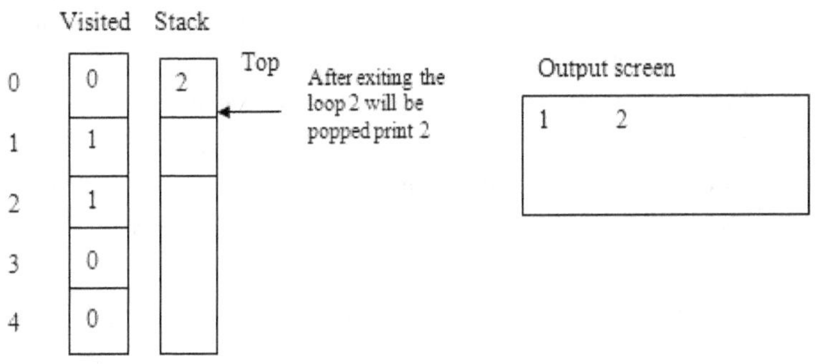

Step 2: Find adjacent vertex to 1, say i.e. 2 if it is not visited, 2 will get inserted in the stack, mark it as visited.

Step 3: Find adjacent to 2 i.e. vertex 4 if it is not visited, 4 will get pushed on the stack mark it as visited.

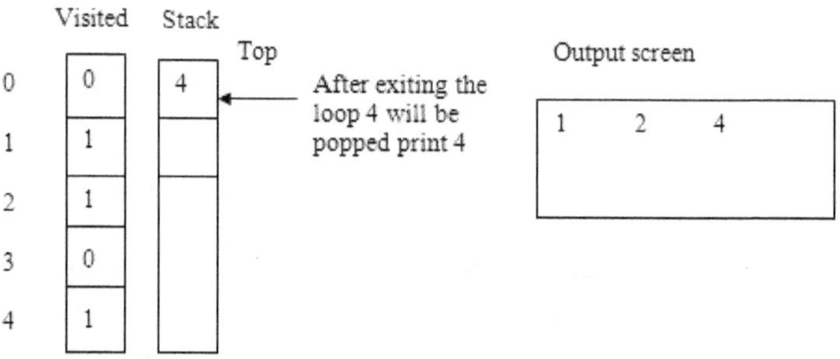

Step 4: Find adjacent to 4 i.e. vertex 3 if it is not visited, 3 will be pushed onto the stack mark it as visited.

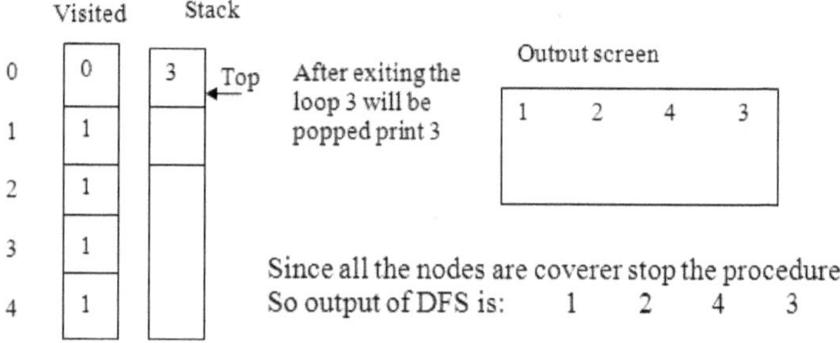

Breadth First Traversal of a Graph

Algorithm

1) Create a graph. Depending on the type of graph i.e. directed or undirected set the value of the flag either 0 or 1 respectively.

2) Read the vertex from which you want to traverse the graph say V_i

3) Initialize the visited array to 1 at the index of V_i.

4) Insert the visited vertex V_i in the queue.

5) Visit the vertex which is at the front of the queue. Delete it from the queue and place its adjacent nodes in the queue.

6) Repeat the step 5, till the queue is not empty.

7) Stop.

Explanation of Logic of BFS Program

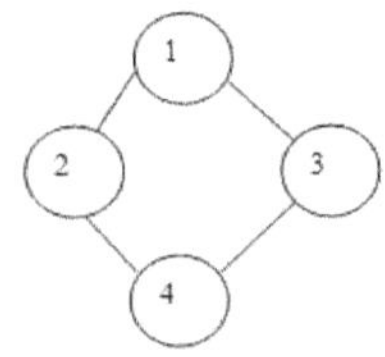

In BFS queue is maintained for storing the adjacent nodes and an array 'visited' is maintained for keeping the track of visited nodes. i.e., once a particular node is visited it should not be revisited again.

Step 1: Start with vertex 1

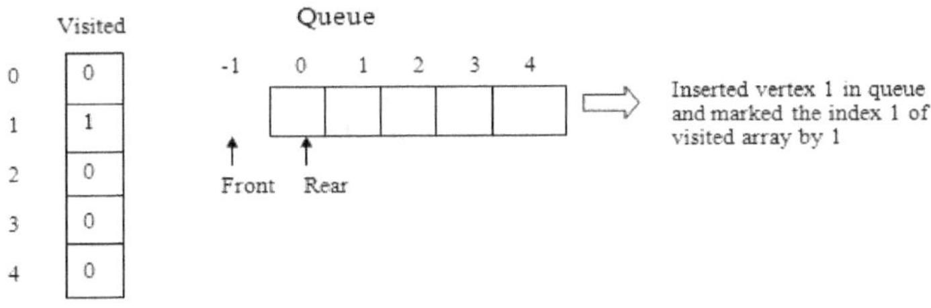

Step 2:

Step 3: Find adjacent vertices of vertex 1 and mark them as visited, insert those in queue. The adjacent vertices of vertex 1 are 2 and 3.

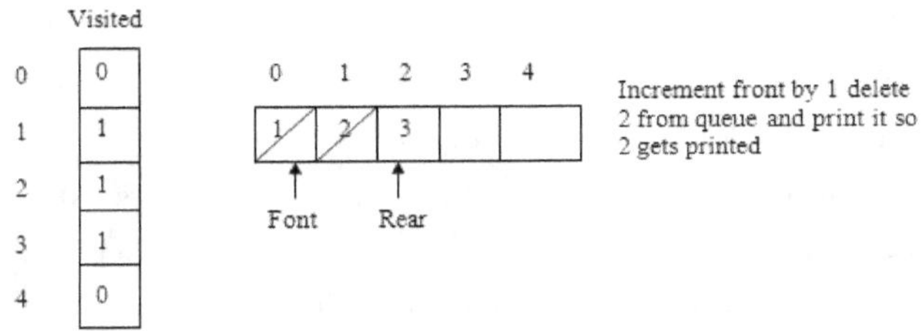

Step 4: Find adjacent to 2 and insert those nodes in queue as well as mark them as visited.

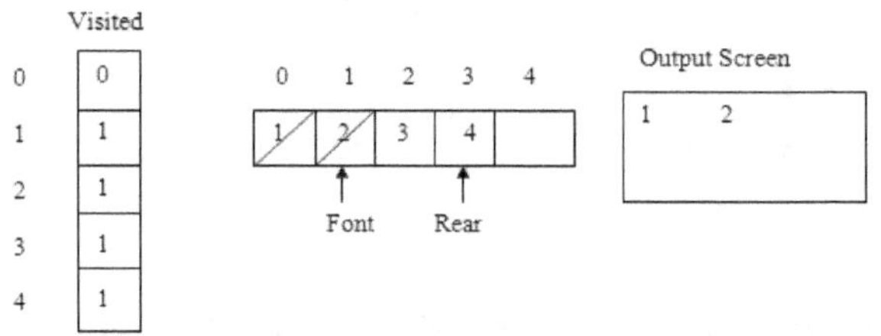

Step 5: Increment front and delete the node print it.

Step 6: find adjacent to 3 i.e. 4 check whether it is marked as visited. If it is marked as visited don't insert in the queue.

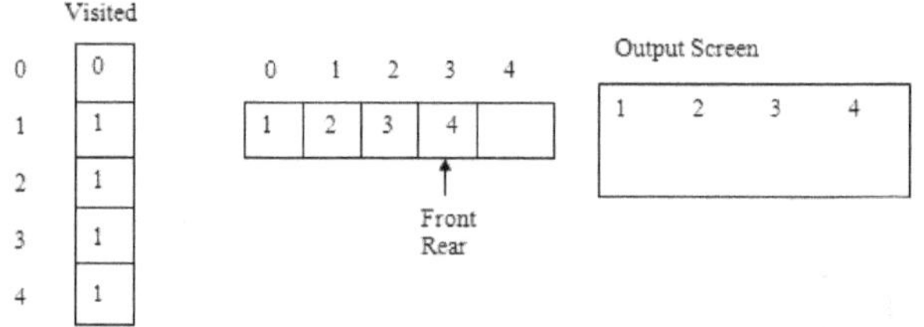

Increment front, delete the node form the queue and print it.

So output will be- BFS for above graph is: 1   2   3   4

Applications of Graph

1) In computer networking such as local area network (LAN), wide area networking (WAN), internetworking.

2) In telephone cabling graph theory is effectively used.

3) In job scheduling algorithms, graphs are used.

Since graph is nothing but the collection of nodes (vertices) and edges. One can find the best-suited distance within the vertices. If the distance between the two vertices is reduced then the cost of cabling and the time in traveling through the nodes will get reduced. .

Definition of Spanning Tree

A spanning tree is a subset of a tree T in which all the vertices of tree T are present but it may not contain all the edges.

The minimum spanning tree of a weighted connected graph G is called minimum spanning tree if its weight is minimum. There are two popular algorithms are used to construct minimum spanning tree, namely prim's algorithm and kruskal's algorithm.

1. **Prim's algorithm:** in prim's algorithm the pair with the minimum weight is to be chosen. Then adjacent to these vertices whichever is the edge having minimum weight is selected. This process will be continued till all the vertices are not been covered.

    For example consider the following graph:

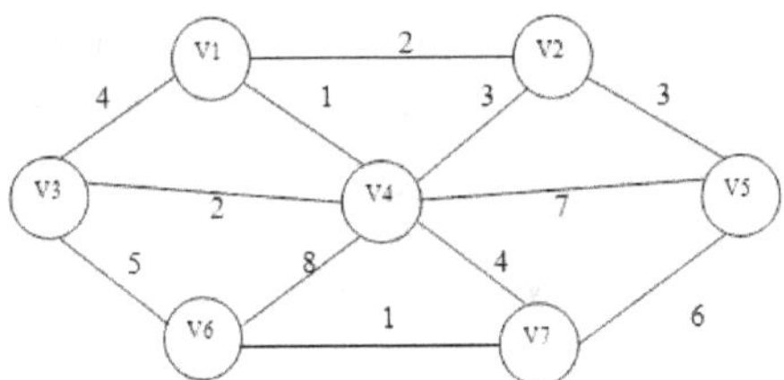

Prim's algorithm can be explained with the help of prim's table. The initial configuration is shown below.

V	Known	d_v	p_v
V1	0	0	0
V2	0	∞	0
V3	0	∞	0
V4	0	∞	0
V5	0	∞	0
V6	0	∞	0
V7	0	∞	0

For each vertex we keep values d_v and p_v and an indication of whether it is known or unknown. D_v is the weight of the shortest arc connecting to v to a known vertex, and p_v, as before, is the last vertex to cause a change in d_v.

Initially v1 is selected and v2,v3,v4 are updated. The table shown below after v1 is declared as known vertex.

V	Known	d_v	p_v
V1	1	0	0
V2	0	2	V1
V3	0	4	V1
V4	0	1	V1
V5	0	∞	0
V6	0	∞	0
V7	0	∞	0

The table after v1 is declared known

The next vertex selected is v4. Every vertex adjacent to v4. v1 is not examined because it is known. V2 is unchanged, because it has $d_v = 2$ and the edge cost from v4 to v2 is 3; all the rest are updated. This shown in the below table.

V	Known	d_v	p_v
V1	1	0	0
V2	0	2	V1
V3	0	2	V4
V4	1	1	V1
V5	0	7	V4
V6	0	8	V4
V7	0	4	V4

The table after v4 s declared known

The next vertex chosen is v2. This does not affect any distances. Then v3 is chosen, which affects the distance in v6, producing results from the selection of v7, which forces v6 and v5 to be adjusted. Finally V6 and v5 are selected.

V	Known	d_v	p_v
V1	1	0	0
V2	1	2	V1
V3	1	2	V4
V4	1	1	V1
V5	0	7	V4
V6	0	5	V3
V7	0	4	V4

The table after v2 and then v3 are declared known

V	Known	d_v	p_v
V1	1	0	0
V2	1	2	V1
V3	1	2	V4
V4	1	1	V1
V5	0	6	V7
V6	0	1	V7
V7	1	4	V4

The table after v7 is declared known

V	Known	d_v	p_v
V1	1	0	0
V2	1	2	V1
V3	1	2	V4
V4	1	1	V1
V5	0	6	V7
V6	0	1	V7
V7	0	4	V4

The table after v6 and v5 are selected (prim's algorithm terminates)

The edges in the spanning tree can be read from the table: (v2,v1), (v3,v4), (v4,v1), (v5,v7), (v6,v7), (v7,v4). The total cost is 16.

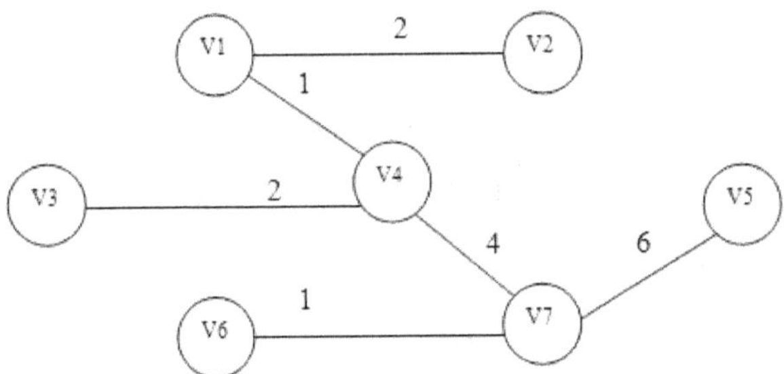

2. **Kruskal's Algorithm:** In Kruskal's algorithm the minimum weight is obtained. In this algorithm also the circuit should not be formed. Each time the edge of weight has to be selected, form the graph. It is not necessary in this algorithm to have edges of minimum weights to be adjacent. Let us solve one example by Kruskal's algorithm.

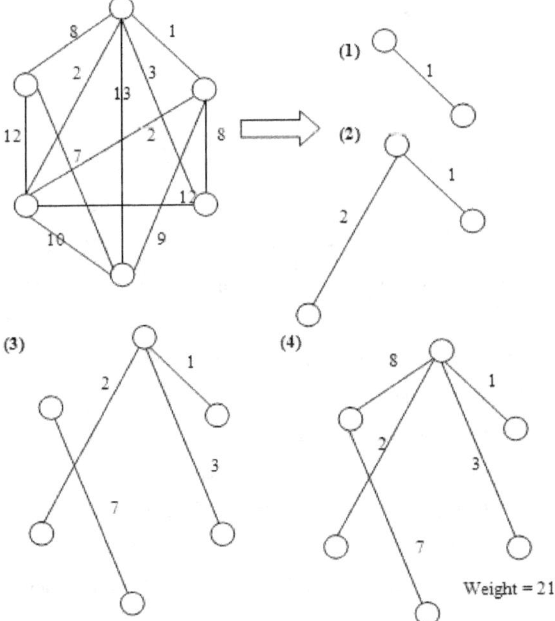

Shortest Path Algorithm

By minimum spanning tree, we are not able to obtain the shortest path between two nodes (source and destination nodes). We can obtain simply the minimum cost. But by using shortest path algorithm we can obtain the minimum distance between two nodes. In our laboratories we have local area network for all the computers. Before designing LAN we should always find out the shortest path and thereby we can obtain economical networking.

There are weighted and un-weighted graph. Based on this category, let us discuss the shortest path algorithm.

1. **Un-weighted shortest path:** the un-weighted shortest path algorithm gives a path in un-weighted graph which is equal to number of edges traveled from source to destination.

   For Example: Consider the Graph Given Below

   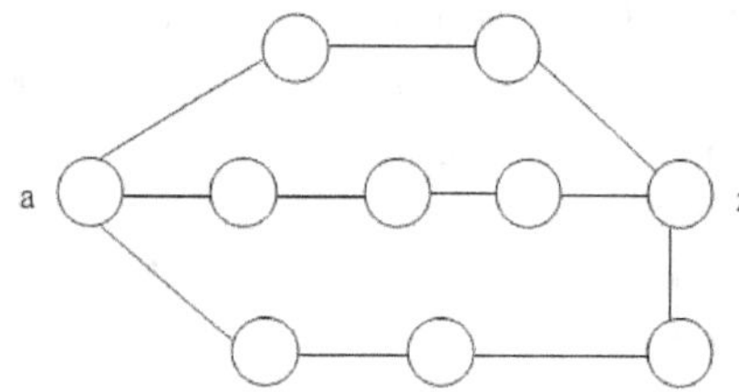

   The paths between a to z are as below:

Sr.No	Path	Number of edges
1	V1-v2-v3-v10	3
2	V1-v4-v5-v6-10	4
3	V1-v7-v8-v9-v10	4

   Out of these the path 1 i.e. v1-v2-v3-v10 is shortest one as it consists of only 3 edges from a to z

2. **Dijkstra's shortest path algorithm:** the Dijkstra's shortest path algorithm suggests the shortest path from some source node to the some other destination node. The source node or the node from we start measuring the distance is called the start node and the destination node is called the end node. In this algorithm we start finding the distance from the start node and find the all the paths from it to neighboring nodes. Among those whichever is the nearest node that path is selected. This process of finding the nearest node is repeated till the end node. Then whichever is the path that path is called the shortest path.

For Example: Consider the Graph Given Below

P = set which is for nodes which have already selected

T = remaining node

Step 1: v = a

P ={2}   T = {b,c,d,e,f,z}

Dist (b) = min{old dist(b), dist(a)+w(a,b)}

Dist (b) = min{∞,0+22}

Dist (b) = 22

Dist(c) = 16

Dist (d) = 8 (minimum node)

Dist (e) = ∞

Dist (f) = ∞

Dist (z) = ∞

So minimum node is selected in p i.e. node d

Step 2: v = d

P = {a,d}   T = {b,c,e,f,z}

Dist (b) = min{old dist(b),dist(d)+w(b,d)}

Dist (b)=min{22,8+∞}

Dist (b)=22

Dist(c) =min{16,8+10}=16

Dist (e)=min{∞,8+∞}=8

Dist (f)=min{∞,8+6}=14

Dist (z)=min{∞,8+∞}=8

Step 3: v=f

P={a,d,f}   T={b,c,e,z}

Dist (b) = min{22,14+7} = 21

Dist(c) = min{16,14+3} = 16

Dist (e) = min{∞,14+∞} = ∞

Dist (z) = min(∞,14+9} = 23

Step 4: v = c

P = {a,d,f,c}   T = {b,e,z}

Dist (b) = min{21,16+20} = 21

Dist (e) = min(∞,16+4} = 20

Dist (z) = min{23,16+10} = 23

Step 5: v= e

P={a,d,f,c,e}   T={b,z}

Dist (b) = min{21,20+2} = 21

Dist (z) = min{23,20+4} = 23

Step 6: v=b

P={a,d,f,c,e,b}   T = {z}

Dist (z) = min{23,21+2} = 23.

Now the target vertex for finfing the shortest path is z. hence the length of the shortest path from the vertex a to z is 23.

The shortest path is as shown below:

Bi-Connectivity

Bi-connected graphs are the graphs which cannot be broken into two disconnected pieces (graphs) by connecting single edge. For example

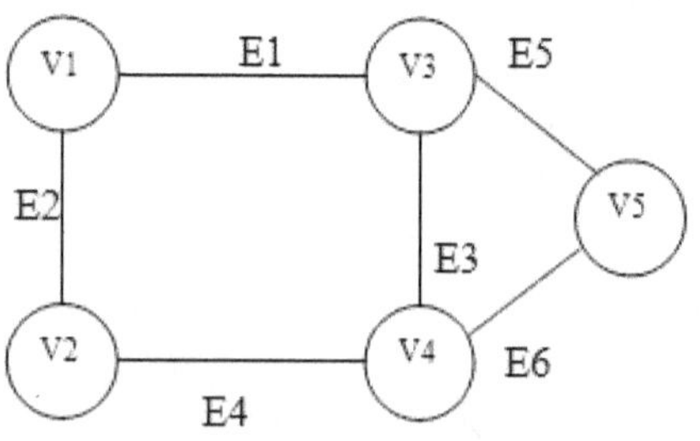

In the given figure even if we remove any single edge the graph does not become disconnected.

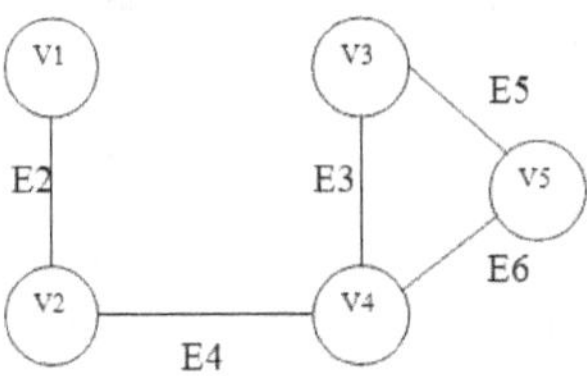

For example even if we remove an edge E1 the graph does not become disconnected. We do not get two disconnected components of graph.

Properties of Bi-Connected Graph

1. There are two disjoint paths between any two vertices
2. There exists simple between two vertices
3. There should not be any cut vertex (cut vertex is a vertex which if we remove then the graph becomes disconnected)

Introduction to NP completeness problem

For Obtaining Solution to Any Problem there are Two Classes Defined

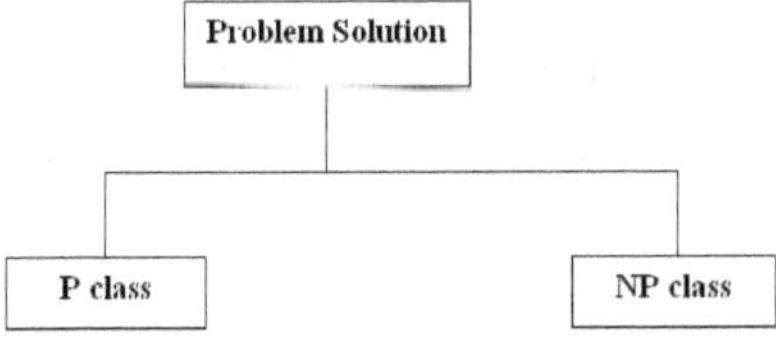

1) P class (Polynomial Time Class)

P is a class of problems which could be solved deterministically (definitely) in a polynomial time. The term polynomial time means the time which is function of polynomial(x). that means the polynomial time = coef * x^i

Where I= 0 to N.

If N=0, then polynomial time = constant

If N=1, then polynomial time=x

If N=2, then polynomial time=x^2

And so on that means in sample terms polynomial time is linear time or, square time or cubic time and so on.

2) NP Class (Non Deterministic Polynomial Time Class)

NP completeness problem is a class of problems for which we can make out the guess of solution of these problems which will get solved in polynomial time.

For example:

Traveling salesman's problem

The traveling salesman's problem can be stated as follows. A traveling salesman wants to traverse a path such that he starts at vertex V_0 (we can even call each vertex as a city) and visits every other vertex exactly once finally returns to vertex V_0. Find out the minimum path length.

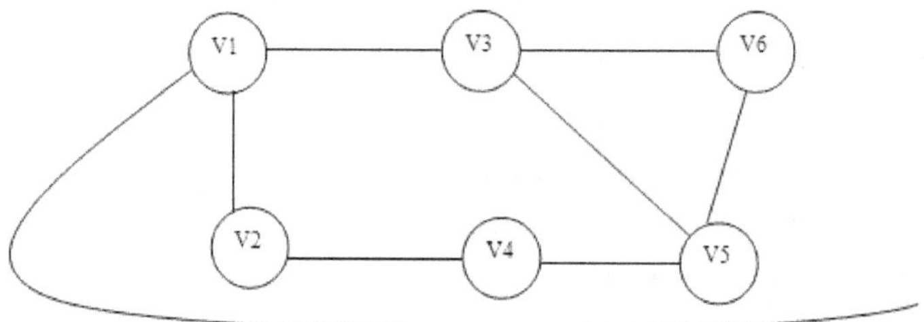

This problem is NP complete problem. For the above graph we cannot deterministically find out solution, such a solution which will be executable in polynomial time.

Hamiltonian problem: a Hamiltonian problem can be stated as follows. A graph is posses Hamiltonian cycle if we can traverse it starting from vertex V_0 visits every vertex exactly once and returns to vertex V_0.

For example:

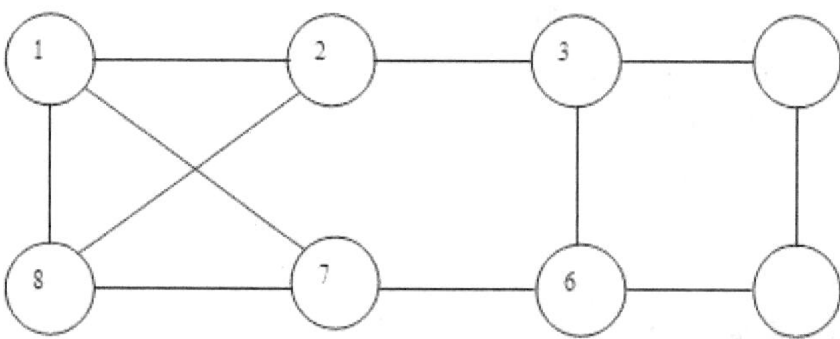

The Hamiltonian cycle will be 1-2-8-7-6-5-4-3-1. The Hamiltonian problem is also NP complete problem. As we can simply make a guess of solution which will get executed in polynomial time.